UNVEILING THE MYSTERY OF THE BLOOD OF JESUS

The Life-Changing Significance of the Cross

David S. Philemon

Royal Diadem Publishing Inc.

UNVEILING THE MYSTERY OF THE BLOOD OF JESUS
The Life-Changing Significance of the Cross
978-1-966141-38-9

For permissions, additional information, or bulk order inquiries, please
contact the author.

Write:
Royal Diadem Publishing Inc.
4836 W. 13th Street, Cicero, IL 60804
1 (312) 970-0183

Unless otherwise indicated, all Scripture quotations in this volume are taken
from the King James Version (KJV) and the New King James Version (NKJV) of
the Holy Bible.

To the Lamb of God, whose shed blood speaks mercy, peace, and strength to all who seek refuge in Him. To every believer who has experienced the transformative power of Jesus's blood, may this book deepen your understanding and ignite a fresh passion for our Savior. To those seeking redemption and freedom, may the mystery of the blood reveal God's love and guide you into the abundance of His grace. Apostle Dr. David Philemon

ACKNOWLEDGMENT

I extend my heartfelt gratitude to: My Lord and Savior, Jesus Christ, whose blood is the source of all wisdom, inspiration, and life.

My family, whose unwavering support and prayers have been a constant source of strength.

My fellow laborers in the Kingdom, whose shared passion for the Gospel, have fueled this endeavor.

The faithful men and women have walked alongside me to offer guidance, encouragement, and valuable insights.

The publishers, editors, and designers who have skillfully crafted this book for the benefit of readers everywhere.

May this work honor the Lord Jesus Christ and bless all who seek to understand the mystery of His precious blood

Apostle Dr. David Philemon

CONTENTS

INTRODUCTION

The Chrisom Thread

T he Chrisom Thread, symbolizing the anointing and life-giving power of Jesus' blood, represents the divine filament that weaves together mercy, energy, and transformation. This sacred thread connects heaven's throne to humanity's deepest needs, carrying power and authority that flows from God's mercy seat in heaven.

As a result, the blood of Jesus Christ can bring multiple levels of transformation and deliverance when humanly understood. This is possible because the blood spilled on Calvary's cross achieved monumental victories, annihilating Satan's works and exalting God's purposes in our lives.

"And they overcame him by the blood of the Lamb" (Revelation 12:11, KJV). When Satan designs ungodly plans, pleading the blood of Jesus in faith collapses these schemes, canceling curses, hexes, spells, voodoo, and evil sacrifices. Every chain is broken, and God turns evil intentions into blessings for His children (Genesis 50:20).

The blood also purges our conscience and hearts from the works of the flesh, preparing us to accommodate the Holy Spirit. *"How much more shall the blood of Christ...purge your conscience from dead works to serve the living God?"* (Hebrews 9:14, KJV). It washes away guilt, shame, and condemnation, securing abundant living.

With confident assurance, every child of God is protected under the sacrificial blood, complete before Him from all sins. The blood raises visions, dreams, and life purposes beyond human strength.

As Scripture affirms, *"For as the rain cometh down...So shall my word be that goeth forth out of my mouth"* (Isaiah 55:10-11, KJV), the blood hallows projects and clears paths for divine accomplishment. The previously distant or unimaginable becomes possible through divine speed.

Engaging the blood of Jesus is crucial, as it *"speaks better things than the blood of Abel"* (Hebrews 12:24, KJV), testifying to mercy, peace, and strength. Invoking the blood reminds us of Christ's ultimate sacrifice and aligns us with His victory.

The blood transforms our lives, cleansing us from sin and positioning us for spiritual growth. It empowers us to live purposefully, overcome obstacles, and align with God's will.

This book unveils the profound mystery of Christ's blood in a magnificent tapestry of insight. As you read, let your heart be open to these revelations from God.

CHAPTER ONE

THE POWER OF THE BLOOD OF JESUS

Most people don't realize how crucial Jesus' death, burial, and resurrection are to the Christian faith. Since the fall of man in the Garden of Eden, life has become so weak that whenever evil appears, it often seems more substantial than good. Whether you like it or not, when Adam and Eve sinned, they planted sin in the earth and severed our fellowship with God. God told Adam, "If you eat this fruit, in dying, you shall die." From the moment man disobeys God and eats, everything begins to die.

The 'fall' handed Satan the authority of the earth while putting man in a position where he has to seek God's mercy. But God, in His infinite wisdom, had plans to restore this relationship, and the best way for Him to do that was to become a man. So, Jesus isn't just some historical figure - He's the Son of God in human flesh. So, God planned to restore this relationship, and it wasn't just some half-baked idea. No, He decided to become a man but remained God. Apostle Paul said in 1 Timothy 3:16 (KJV): *"And without controversy great is the mystery of godliness: God was manifest in the flesh, justified in the Spirit, seen of angels, preached unto the Gentiles, believed on in the world, received up into glory."* Do you see what I'm getting at? Jesus is God who became a man to cover the gap between humanity and divinity, between the earthly and the heavenly.

Now, when I talk about the blood of Jesus, I'm not just talking about some physical substance. I'm talking about something more significant than any earthly power. It's God's provision for humanity, the vicarious atonement of Christ. That blood that gushed out on the cross? It's holy and mortal, and it cleanses us from sins.

Look at it this way: Jesus arose from the dead to show us the supremacy of His victory. His blood dismantled Satan's grip on the fallen man. Those who believe in the redeeming work of Jesus Christ? They receive new, eternal life as God's children. That's not something to take lightly.

When we sing about Jesus' blood and its power, we reflect on what our Lord and Savior sacrificed. He gave His life to pull us back from the arms of sin, which resulted in his death. Without that sacrifice, we couldn't possibly cohabit with the Lord. That blood allows us to fellowship with our Father in heaven now and in the future.

The power in that blood is accurate, and it's life-changing. It's a shield against evil in this world. It's strength when we're under attack. It even affects our physical bodies, restoring damaged organs. Remember what Isaiah 53:5 (NKJV) says? *"But he was wounded for our transgressions; he was bruised for our iniquities; the chastisement of our peace was upon him; and with his stripes, we are healed."*

And it doesn't stop there. The blood of Jesus purges our conscience of guilt, sanctifies and justifies us, and gives us the boldness to approach God's throne of grace. We can pray for favor and commit different situations to the blood of Jesus because we believe it can influence all circumstances.

So, don't take this for granted. The blood of Jesus is the living God's power given to believers to walk in dominion. Just as blood supports our physical bodies, the blood of Christ is a life-supporting power to all who trust in Him. It's not just about believing - it's about living in the power of that blood every single day. That's the real power of the blood of Jesus.

The Blood Speaks

These words speak don't mean talking. This is not just verbal musing or a sign of a past event. It's something the Bible says is happening right now, even as we speak: the precious blood of Jesus Christ shed on that cross. It has a message and speaks of mercy, strength, peace, and protection.

The world is a whole of hate and sin; the blood of Jesus is whispering compassion and forgiveness. Nothing's beyond repair of the blood; no matter how deep you've dug yourself, there's a way out. The blood. It's shouting about a love beyond measure, a complete forgiveness that wipes out every sin.

Think about it—we've all messed up, and we get our chance to give a less-than-stellar performance. But here's the thing: the blood of Jesus is not pointing fingers. It's justifying us. Hebrews 9:22 (KJV) says: "*And almost all things are by the law purged with blood, and without shedding of blood is no remission.*" That blood speaks mercy, offering us a clean slate.

But it's not just mercy. The blood has a message of strength, too. Life's tough, right? We've got troubles, problems, and times when we're ready to throw in the towel. That's when the blood of Jesus speaks strength into our weary hearts. It's saying, "Don't give up. Someone's fighting for you where you can't."

This strength isn't about muscling through on your own. It's the kind that comes from deep in your soul, knowing you're standing on God's power. Ephesians 6:10 (KJV) nails it: "*Finally, my brethren, be strong in the Lord and the power of his might.*" The blood of Jesus is empowering us to face life head-on.

Everything is becoming crazy today; our world is full of chaos and conflict, but the blood of Jesus is speaking peace. Not the kind that pretends problems don't exist, but the kind that stands firm in the storm. It's not just about feeling calm. It's knowing that nothing can make God let go of you. The blood's telling us the war's already won. Colossians 1:20 (KJV) puts it beautifully: "*And, having made peace through the blood of his cross, by him to reconcile all things unto himself; by him, I say, whether they be things in earth or things in heaven.*"

A lot of folks don't get how valuable peace is. Jesus told his disciples, "*Peace I leave with you; my peace I give unto you; not as the world giveth, give I unto you. Let not your heart be troubled, nor let it be afraid.*" John 14:27 KJV. People's fears? They're real. But you've got a choice: embrace peace and trust God, or let fear take over. Peace breeds courage, my friend. It's a gift.

And protection? The blood's speaking that, too. The blood of Jesus is like armor. It's not just about keeping your body safe (though it can do that). It's guarding your spirit. Remember the Passover? Exodus 12:12-13, the Israelites put lamb's blood on their doors, and the destroyer passed over. God told Moses to use that blood as protection. And you know what? If an Egyptian had done the same, they'd have been saved too. When you're under the blood of Jesus, you're preserved.

So what does this look like day to day? When guilt drags you down, the blood shouts, "Forgiven!" When you're worn out and ready to quit, the blood's saying, "Keep going!" When worry's got you in a chokehold, the blood whispers, "Peace," and calms your heart. And when you're scared and feeling exposed? The blood's right there saying, "I've got you covered." This isn't ancient history or some dusty religion. The blood of Christ is alive and kicking today, working in believers' lives all over the world.

We've got to listen. The blood's speaking, but are we tuning in? Are we letting its message of mercy, strength, peace, and protection shape our thoughts, actions, and lives? Can you imagine waking up knowing the blood of Jesus is on you! Through every struggle, decision, interaction—it's there offering mercy when you mess up, strength when you're weak, peace when you're worried, and protection when you're scared.

So how do we tap into this? It starts with belief, my friend. We've got to have faith in the blood Jesus shed. Then we've got to declare it. Speak it out. Remind yourself what the blood's saying about you and your standing with God. When you're feeling condemned, say it: "The blood cleanses me." When weakness hits, declare: "The blood gives me strength." Anxiety creeping in? Remember: "The blood speaks peace to my heart." Feeling vulnerable? Proclaim: "The blood of Christ protects me and mine."

The blood of Jesus isn't just history or doctrine. It's a living, breathing word for today. It's pardoning compassion, sustaining power, comforting peace, and unbreakable protection. When we start really listening to what the blood's saying, we'll live fuller, freer lives. So today, tomorrow, every day—let's tune in to what the blood's saying. Let's take that message we desperately need and let it change how we live. Because when the blood speaks, it's all about life, hope, and victory. And that, my friend, is a message we all need to hear.

The Divine Voice Of The Blood

The blood has a voice, which is an idea that goes to the essence of Christianity; it provides an analysis of the complex message of salvation and forgiveness. When we use words like the blood of Jesus is speaking, it is not a poetic language we are using; it is a spiritual language that works.

We should first see what the Bible has to say on this matter. In Hebrews 12: But Hebrews 12:24 (KJV) says, *"And to Jesus the mediator of the new covenant, and to the blood of sprinkling, that speaketh better things than that of Abel."* This makes an outstanding contrast of the blood of Jesus and Abel, the first recorded victim of murder in the holy scriptures.

The brother's blood of Abel called for vengeance and vendetta. It was a cry of death that should not be. But the blood of Jesus? It refers to something much broader than that. It talks about compassion, pardon, and restoration. What Abel's blood called for is vengeance, while that of Jesus speaks of forgiveness.

This isn't just an example of theological wordplay. It is then a major change in the paradigm whereby we comprehend the word of God. The blood of Jesus speaks better things because it goes further than just pointing out sin—it lays down the cure. Not only does it make sin stand out; it shows a path to liberation.

So, what does it mean for the blood to "speak"? It is not the actual words that can be heard with the ears but the spiritual reality of what the blood of Jesus does. It speaks, as it does when it declares; when it bears witness to a new revelation of who we are or of how God sees us.

Think about it this way: when you have sinned and are laden with guilt or shame, the blood of Jesus is there, declaring over you a better thing. It's announcing that you are accepted and clean from your sin. It's declaring all your sorrows will turn to joy, your liabilities will turn to assets, and your dead will arise from the grave.

Revelation 12:11. Here there is the blood of Jesus not only making a discourse but also gives victory to the believers. It is a living power that is the deliverer from the foe and makes us stable in our faith. But you may be asking yourself, "How do I make this real in my life?" How can I make the blood cry on my behalf? Great question! Here are some practical ways to tap into the power of the blood of Jesus:

- *Declare it daily*: Every morning begin by speaking aloud affirmations regarding the efficacy of the blood. Like, utter the following, "Today, the blood of Jesus stands for me." It tells me that I am forgiven, righteous, beloved, etc."

- *Apply it in prayer*: As you pray, purposely try to "rub in" the blood of Jesus to your circumstances. For example, Lord, I stand on the blood of Jesus for my health, my relationships, my job, and so on.
- *Use it in spiritual warfare*: If you are tested or you are under spiritual trial, plead the blood." As a faithful Christian, I take authority in the name of Jesus to cover my mind, the emotional side, and my decision-making with the blood."
- *Meditate on its meanings*: Focus on what the blood of Jesus represents—forgiveness, cleansing, protection, etc. Take these facts into the very center of your being.
- *Take communion regularly*: The act of communion is a strong call for the value of blood as a symbol. Take the time to concentrate on what Jesus did and achieved.
- *Sing about it*: Several hymns and worship songs have brought the topic of Jesus's blood to the limelight. These can be sung, which makes them effective in driving home some of the messages that are part of the process.
- *Share its power*: Share the testimony this blood has worked in your life. Your testimony can simply let the blood testify to something to other people.

Bear in mind it's not just about the blood that was shed on the cross 2000 years ago, but blood being shed now. It's about a force that is alive and real and operating in your life at this point. Whenever you are being accused, the blood cries out for you and testifies for your innocence. Every instance of the power of sin being felt when aspiring to be holy, the blood of Jesus declares you free. Anytime the brain tells you that you are helpless, worthless, or unwanted, the blood screams your worth.

One must remember that this is not an overnight magic. It's all about trust—trusting in the completed work of Calvary. That is never our purpose when we shout the blood of Jesus; we are not aiming to pull a fast one over God or make some sort of Joe Friday call-in. We are just starting to ourselves (and the spiritual realm) what is already factual given Jesus' act.

When it comes to the latter one, the divine voice of the blood is always speaking. It's telling you that you are forgiven, that you are redeemed, and that you have been given authority and dominion over your life. It is the shout of victory, healing, and freedom, which is your reality and expression of what God has done in your life. The task of the marketing community is to listen in, to listen carefully, and to get in sync.

So today, and every day, let the blood of Jesus speak for you. Let it silence the voices of condemnation, fear, and doubt. Let it drown out the accusations of the enemy. And let it speak loud and clear the truth of who you are in Christ - beloved, redeemed, and victorious.

The blood of Jesus truly does speak better things. It speaks of a love so profound it can forgive any sin, a power so great it can overcome any obstacle, and a grace so amazing it can transform any life. That's the divine voice of the blood - and it's speaking for you right now.

The Role Of The Blood In Favor And Preservation

The blood of Jesus as an agent of favor as well as divine protection represents depth and strength. Not only an article of faith, but an experience that can impel a conversion of our everyday practices into living ones. First, let's try to understand what favor really means. In the Bible, favor can best be defined as God's mercy on us, His willingness to bless us in ways that we do not deserve. And the blood of Jesus has an important role to play in all this. What Jesus did was offer the people a way to appear before God and not be seen as sinners but as children.

In Psalms 5:12 KJV it says, "*For thou, LORD, wilt bless the righteous; with favor wilt thou compass him as with a shield.*" The blood of Jesus provides us with acceptance and favor of God. Divine favor is a major spiritual force that forces your day to bring joy and gladness to you. When favor is at work labor is reduced. *What favor can do in 10 days' labor cannot do in 10 years*. (Psalm 5:12 Psalms. 68:19-20)

I mean to ponder—the blood of Jesus is a reference to our salvation. It makes the pronouncement that the price tag for our sins has been met in its fullness. Because of this, we can approach God with confidence, not because it is some divine endure but because it is guaranteed that we are accepted. This is the very nature of divine favor: to be in a place where God is pleased to bless, not because of what we are or what we have done, but because of the work of Christ.

This favor shows up in different forms in our lives. It might manifest in the form of coincidences, divine appointments, or divine intervention in the form of provision. That is one of those things to have in life, like having a wind that pushes you forward. However, do not forget that favor is not a life of no problems, no challenges, but to have God on your side as you face those challenges.

Jesus' blood does not only open doors for us but also protects our lives from any evil. Like the angel who passed over the houses that had the blood of the Passover Lamb on their doorposts, like the angel of death passed over all those houses that did not have the blood of the Passover Lamb, so we are shielded from eternal death by the blood of Jesus, the Passover Lamb.

Revelation 12:11 helps me realize that the blood of Jesus is one of the tools we have with which to fight each day against the enemy.

This divine shield is not solely spiritual (even though it can be). It is about being safe regarding the soul, the heart, and the brain. What the blood of Jesus does is that it forms a wall through which the enemy cannot cross. They protect us from delusion, from hatred, and from hopelessness.

But as you hear this, how does it play out in real life? What can be done to bring this favor and protection into our existence in everyday lives? Here are some key ways:

- *Plead the Blood*: It's not about begging but about proclaiming the blood over your life. In the morning, for instance, you might wake up and say the following: I plead the blood of Jesus over my life, my family, my desk, everything that concerns me.
- *Take Communion Regularly*: Communion is a symbolic act that can call to mind what the blood of Jesus has done. It's a way of being included in the redeeming aspect of what Christ did on the cross through the body.
- *Act on It*: Walk in the consciousness that you are chosen and, therefore, shielded. This might mean acting in faith, moving forward and taking godly risks, or withstanding the pressures when faced with opposition.
- *Thank God for It*: They should learn to express thankfulness for the favor and protection offered by the blood from time to time. This is a way of keeping you always in touch with its potential and productivity in your existence.
- *Share It*: Inform others about how you have been favored and protected in life through the blood of Jesus. Testimonies remind other people of the power of faith and strengthen our own faith.

Please do not forget that the blood does not cease to work its power; it is a daily phenomenon! In the everyday and in all circumstances, the blood of Jesus is declaring favor and protection for your life. It's stepping out and saying that you belong, that you matter, and that you're worthy of being defended.

This doesn't mean you will not experience situations that

challenge or pose a threat to your life at some point. But it does mean that you confront them knowing you are on the right side of God and that he has your back.

Did you begin the previous day with such confidence that, no matter what happened, it happens to you when you are walking in God's favor and your God shields you? How would that alter how you negotiate the contingencies encountered in one's day-to-day life? In what way would it change your self-esteem, choices, and interactions?

The blood of Jesus is not a mere symbol but blood—human blood. It's here and now—it's alive; it's a part of your current life experience. It is taking you into a position where God loves to bless you most. It's offering you armor that shields you from the enemy's plan.

Therefore, today and every day, let the blood of Jesus continue to write favor and protection over your life. Let it remind you that you're not alone in dealing with life or that you have got heaven in your back. Step out with the assurance of a divine endorsement in the blood of Jesus, knowing He remains your shield and your defender.

Permanent Victory Through The Blood

I believe every believer has recognized how permanent, strong and powerful is the blood of Jesus when it comes to our everyday victory over the forces of darkness and sin. The blood of Jesus, through the process of crucifixion, did not only deliver a quick fix to our problems; instead, it brought an eternal victory over the devil. But here's the key: although this victory is eternal in kind, perhaps our construct's enjoyment of this triumph is contingent upon the continuous recitation and integration of the blood into our everyday schedules.

Before getting down to the details of this victory, we can start with what the Bible has to say about the subject. Revelation 12:11(APMC)

"And they have overcome (conquered) him by means of the blood of the Lamb and by the utterance of their testimony, for they did not love and cling to life even when faced with death [holding their lives cheap till they had to die for their witnessing]."

The blood of Jesus is a vital weapon in our spiritual battle, which allows us to overcome the enemy. He said we conquered him by the means of the blood. The victory that the blood brings is eternal. It cannot be re-won or the constant reinforcement of which has to be embarked on. When Jesus said on the cross, *"It is finished"* (John 19:30, KJV), He was proclaiming a victory over sin, death, and the devil in its entirety and once and for all. It does not require winning some of the battles or winning those battles for some time—it must win every conflict and must win it forever.

But our contribution to this victory is inevitable. Namely, the experience of the battle and the everyday use of such triumph are not eternal; they need to be constantly actively incorporated by the contending side. Strength for Growth is the same way—one doesn't lose strength, but at the same time, one has to pick it up as a weapon and benefit from what God has offered.

Therefore, why is it necessary to always invoke the blood? Recalling the blood has the power to assert the believer's identity based on the gospel summons—we are Christians, and thus we are warriors; we are kings and queens in Christ Jesus! The devil is always on the prowl, looking for the best opportunity to attack our trust and rob us of our joy. The blood is, therefore, invoked as a strong way of resisting these attacks.

To speak about the blood is to bring our minds into subjection to the reality of what has been done by Christ." Every time we use the blood, we exercise faith, which is our body's spiritual muscle.

How Can We Practically Invoke The Blood For Continual Triumph?

Begin every morning saying to yourself, I am protected by the blood of Jesus. There, by His blood, is my victory!" When tempted, say, for instance, by temptations of sin, utter, 'Through the blood, I have authority over sin. I choose victory."

No matter what happens, speak these words out loud. "The blood of Jesus has won my victory. It rightly said, 'I walk in victory despite what I see.' If you are up to being under spiritual attack, say this: Jesus' blood is against every attack from the enemy. I stand victorious." Pray this prayer often: "I use the written word and the blood of Jesus to divide my life, family, and possessions."

Once again, it should be clear that invoking the blood is not a practice of using keywords or incantations. It is so simple yet profound—it is about faith, faith in the finished work of Christ. Every time we mention the blood, we are, therefore, taking our stand to affirm to ourselves (and the realm of the spirit) what Christ has done.

The victory secured through Jesus' shed blood is eternal and absolute. Our role is not to re-fight this battle, but to periodically invoke and align with its power. By doing so, we'll walk in a realm of triumph that transforms our personal lives and the world around us.

Thus, you must remember today and every day, the eternal triumph in Christ. Let's do this consistently: consecrate, invoke, and empower His blood. And let's live with that victory that is ours, through Jesus the Christ through what He did at the cross

CHAPTER TWO

UNLOCKING THE HIDDEN DIMENSIONS OF THE BLOOD

T he blood of Jesus that was spilt on Calvary is much more than a historical occurrence or a symbol of Christianity. He made it alive and active, which are nowadays having a positive impact in the lives of Christians. There is no length that the blood cannot go for the believer's benefit, no limit to the blood's potential and usefulness.

The blood of Jesus, is a spiritual currency. It's got value beyond anything we can imagine. Think about it - what can't the blood do? It cleanses us from sin, it heals our bodies, it protects us from evil, it gives us strength when we're weak. There's no limit to what the blood can accomplish in your life if you'll just believe it and receive it.

In Hebrews 9:22 (KJV), the Bible tells us, "And almost all things are by the law purged with blood; and without shedding of blood is no remission." With this verse we get to know some important fact of our God's redemptive plan: the blood. But that's only the beginning of it. Now in this case, the blood of Jesus is not a remission of sins only, but it also means a new life altogether for believers.

It does not merely sanctify us from sin of flesh; it sanctifies us every day, moment by moment, in the sight of God. Moreover, the implication is that no matter what we go through or how we may sin, the blood can ever be active to cleanse us again. It is like a spiritual shower that is always on, never ceases, and only continues to make us renewed.

But the blood doesn't stop at only cleansing. It also refers to rescue —the act of paying for our freedom from sin and the rights of the devil. This redemption is full and extends to the spirit, soul, and body of man. It means that nothing in our lives is free from the touch of God's saving grace. Whether it's addictions, curses of the generations, or other perversities ingrained into a person from birth.

It even does not include that protective power of the blood, which might also constitute yet another dimension as well. While the blood of the lamb symbolizes the protection on the part of the angel of death in Exodus, the blood of Christ functions as the barrier, the invulnerable coat of armor, the blood of Jesus Christ stands as the wall between believers and destruction. This protection is not only from physical assault (although this is sometimes involved) but from witchcraft, evil spirits, depression, and other such things. When we know and live by this, it is today's walk with no feelings of vulnerability because the supreme power in the world is unfailingly wards off.

There is also another virtue of healing in the blood. The prophet Isaiah declared, "*With his stripes we are healed*" (Isaiah 53:5 KJV), and this healing power is inherent in the blood of Jesus. Not a simple recovery from the physical ailment that involves it, but it is more than that: it includes emotional, mental, and even spiritual healing. There's that element of power in the blood of Jesus that is uniquely capable of healing every aspect of man that is broken, lost, and shattered.

The blood of Jesus also speaks of authority. When we know

how strong the blood is, we know that we have been made rulers and authorities over the kingdom of the darkness. It's not machismo or the Lord of the Rings-like call to spiritual warrior; it's victoriously holding your ground in the victory of Christ. With the blood of Jesus, we know we are backed and can fight the spirit world, attack the kingdoms, and push back the darkness in our lives and society.

There is another hidden feature in the blood, namely that the blood may become holy. It doesn't just save us; it elects us for God's purposes. This sanctifying power then changes us from within, right down to what we desire, and gives us the ability to live holy lives.

The blood of Jesus also gives an invitation. While in the Old Testament, it was scarce for people to see the face of God. But the blood of Jesus has made a way whereby sinners can now stand right before the throne of grace. This means that we can come to God with full assurance because the blood has opened a way for us. When we come in here under the shed of the blood of Jesus, there is no prayer that is too extreme, no prayer that is too crazy.

It is important to consider the reconciling power of the blood. It not only reconciles us to God; it can reconcile even the most estranged of human relationships—the ones even scarred by death. When people really fathom what the blood entails, they are aware that no relationship is beyond repair, no gap too broad to be bridged by the blood of Jesus.

The blood of Jesus also has the power of memory in it. In the communion service, Jesus said, "*This do in remembrance of me*" (1 Corinthians 11:24, KJV). Every time we take communion, we are not merely performing an exercise; we are tapping into the effect of the blood, and with it, the spiritual realm is being reminded of what Christ has done. This act of remembering helps to keep the reality of the blood fresh in our hearts as well as being actively at work.

The blood also has a covenantal dimension. The blood of Jesus actually sealed the new covenant between God and man, a covenant of grace and truth. This covenant relationship also ensures that in Christ, all God's promises are "yes" and "amen." This gives us a legal right in the court above to claim all Christ has bought for us.

Another aspect that cannot be ruled out is the empowering aspect of the blood. It does not only save us; it enables us to become the people that live the Christian life. Through the blood then, there is the same power that raised Christ from the dead with the ability to overcome sin, to have the ability not to sin, and to live a life that is worthy in the sight of God. This empowerment is not a once-off experience but instead an eternal stream of God's power into our existence.

As these dimensions of the blood are considered, one can only begin to imagine that there is no way that the blood is not effective. Jesus' blood has the ability to solve any problem that may seem impossible and address any need that may seem insurmountable. It is the farthest solution for all these human predicaments, the solution for every hunger of the soul.

Strength is found in the blood, but how one feels about it is a different issue; it boils down to a question of belief. This is similar to having a pass to an utterly unlocked credit card yet only using small amounts because we do not know the extent of the limit. The more we receive revelation of what the blood has done, the more we understand how to take it by faith to every part of our lives, and then we will witness more results.

The blood of Jesus has no restrictions on it in everything it does. It permeates every aspect of our lives, meeting every need, defeating every opponent, and sanctifying us unto the Lord Jesus Christ. But as these truths are discovered and used over and over, they will cause us to be experiencing levels of victory, liberty, and power beyond our greatest expectations. The blood of Jesus is an actuality that has the potential to transform everything in and with us. It is my intent to go deeper into what has been purchased by Christ and discover the depth of it.

The Unseen Power Of The Blood

The blood of Jesus Christ is one of the most distinct tools in the hands of Christians, but few harness it to the whole measure. This force pertinent to Christianity, by this statement, is more thoughtful in implications and action than mere symbolism. That is why union with Christ in His sacrifice is not a myth or an idea but a daily opportunity to participate in the divine power when one knows the sacrament.

The Apostle Paul, in his letter to the Ephesians, perfectly expresses the potency of Christ's blood: "*In whom we have redemption through his blood, the forgiveness of sins, according to the riches of his grace;*" (Ephesians 1:7, KJV) This is the fundament power of the blood – redemption, and forgiveness. However, these are merely the starting points of its transformative capabilities.

Most Christians have not even come to an appreciation of the sheer importance of the active involvement of the blood of Jesus in their daily existence. And it is not only history or theology, which is annal or theological truth while present, that can be cited and used as a power for many things in life. The blood of Jesus is not limited to the moment of crucifixion; it is active today and effectively covers the believer in protection, purification, and victory if only the believer activates the power of that blood.

Subtle calls for the blood, omitting it in favor of prayers said out of habit or as part of common practice, start producing fruit in the lives of the believers right away. But once the blood says it and does so deliberately, spiritual effectiveness is raised to a whole new level. When believers start having knowledge regarding the actual application of the blood's power, they can draw on divine strength to change their situations.

The blood of Jesus serves multiple purposes in the life of a believer. In addition to forgiveness, Jesus' blood can cleanse the conscience and wash the inner man, a blot cleaned of any sin. As the blood on the doorposts delivered the Israelites from decimation by the angel of death, so it is the blood of Jesus that provides the believer with oppression by evil forces.

The blood also gives believers the opportunity to draw near to God's nature, knowing that sin had created a barrier between them. The blood of Jesus is one effective weapon in battle against demons or sinners. The blood of Jesus is also associated with healing; this blood is capable of restoring body and soul. The blood makes the believers distinct for God's use and holy living.

Besides being a substance within the Christian faith, the blood of Jesus is performative. When combined with the believer's testimony and selfless devotion, it can become a formidable force against the foe.

For the blood to work fully, the faithful must acquire specific knowledge of its potential. This comes through studying the Scriptures, especially the Old Testament types and New Testament doctrines, and revelation concerning the blood. With knowledge rising, belief in the effectiveness of the blood also intensifies.

The practical application of the blood's power involves Regular confession and repentance, claiming the cleansing power of the blood, verbally applying the blood as a form of spiritual protection over oneself, loved ones, and possessions, invoking the blood during times of temptation or spiritual attack, pleading the blood in prayer for healing and deliverance, and using the blood as a basis for approaching God in worship and intercession.

Believers need to learn to consciously engage the blood of Jesus. By doing so, they will often experience a heightened sense of God's presence, increased effectiveness in prayer, and greater victory over sin and spiritual opposition. The blood becomes not just a knowledge but a lived reality—a constant source of strength and grace in daily endeavors.

It's good to remember that the power is not in the mere repetition of words or in treating the blood as a magical formula. The efficacy of the blood is based on faith and in the finished work of Christ on the cross. Through a genuine, heartfelt dependence on what the blood represents—the life, death, and resurrection of Jesus—its power is manifested.

The world has yet to see the full potential of Jesus's blood unleashed through a body of believers who fully understand and engage its power. As more Christians awaken to this reality and learn to engage the blood consciously and always, we will witness a new era of spiritual demonstration and transformation in the church and society at large.

The unseen power of Jesus's blood remains vast, largely unexplored territory in the spiritual realm. It has the ability to revolutionize a person's life, communities, and even nations. As we delve deeper into this divine mystery, we unlock a source of strength and grace to overcome any challenge and bring about true, lasting transformation.

I have engaged all the dimensions in the blood, and I am telling you that there are things the world is about to witness. The hand of God is about to bring into manifestation things that eyes have not seen, ears have not heard, nor has it entered into the hearts of men. The world is about to experience specific deeper dimensions of the blood of Jesus. The power in the blood that the world is yet to see is about to be revealed extraordinarily.

I am telling you that as I study the things of God, I am learning things; I think that for me, we have come to a place in the body of Christ where the things we learned just to acquire wisdom; God is turning the knowledge, wisdom, and understanding into raw power.

Knowledge is not power but potential power. We have come to a place where everything we know begins to make sense. The more I studied the things of God, the more I started to understand the power of many things, like understanding the power of my connection to God, which can't be explained. You have to experience it. When talking about superpowers, believers are the real supermen and women.

The Blood And Satan's Defeat

Revelations 12:11-12

"They defeated him by the blood sacrifice of the Lamb and by the message of God that they told people. They did not love their lives too much. They were not afraid of death."

The blood of Jesus Christ serves as a solid defense against the enemy's wiles, acting not only as a defensive barrier but also as a powerful force propelling God's agenda forward with unstoppable impetus. This precious blood poured on Calvary's cross holds a potency beyond human comprehension, which cannot only frustrate the adversary's schemes but also raise and amplify the Almighty's magnificent design for His chosen children.

The efficacy of the blood in arresting Satan's machinations is beyond dispute. It serves as a formidable weapon in the arsenal of every believer, capable of dismantling the most intricate plots of darkness. When invoked with faith and understanding, the blood of Jesus becomes an impenetrable shield, deflecting every fiery dart of the wicked one. But its power extends beyond mere defense; it actively advances the Kingdom of God, pushing back the frontiers of darkness and expanding the territories of light.

It said, "And they overcame him by the blood of the Lamb and by the word of their testimony, and *they loved not their lives unto the death*" (Revelation 12:11, KJV). This is the triumphant nature of the blood, showcasing its ability to grant victory over the accuser of the brethren. The blood, coupled with unwavering testimony and selfless devotion, becomes an unstoppable force that repels the enemy and utterly vanquishes him.

The blood of Jesus speaks with an eternal voice, drowning out the adversary's accusations and amplifying God's promises. Its voice declares righteousness where sin once reigned, proclaims healing where sickness had taken root, and announces freedom where bondage had held sway. The blood speaks a better word than that of Abel, as the writer of Hebrews so eloquently puts it: "*And to Jesus the mediator of the new covenant, and to the blood of sprinkling, that speaketh better things than that of Abel*" (Hebrews 12:24, KJV).

This speaking blood does not whisper; it roars with authority, silencing the enemy's lies and magnifying the truth of God's Word. It speaks of redemption, reconciliation, and restoration. It declares the believer righteous, accepted, and beloved. In every situation where Satan seeks to sow discord, the blood speaks peace. Where the enemy attempts to instill fear, the blood proclaims courage. Where darkness threatens to engulf, the blood shines forth as a beacon of inextinguishable light.

The astounding reality is that this blood, so powerful in its effects, is available to every child of God as a perpetual fountain of victory. It is not a resource that diminishes with use but one that multiplies in efficacy with each invocation. The blood deactivates Satan's plans and activates God's plan. Many people are limited because they don't know how to enforce God's plan for their lives. They understand how resist the devil, how to bond demons and cast them out but don't know how to enforce the plan and purpose of God for their lives. Therefore, the exhortation stands: never grow weary of invoking the blood. It is our irrevocable license for permanent triumph, our unassailable guarantee of continuous conquest over the forces of darkness.

In the realm of spiritual warfare, the blood of Jesus emerges as the ultimate weapon, more potent than any strategy the enemy can devise. The blood is one of the most effective tools for spiritual warfare. It dismantles strongholds, breaks generational curses, and shatters the chains of addiction and oppression. When applied with faith, it creates an atmosphere where demonic forces cannot operate, establishing a zone of divine dominion where God's purposes flourish unhindered.

Moreover, the blood of Jesus serves as a catalyst for supernatural blessings. It opens doors that were once firmly shut, grants favor in impossible situations, and releases an outpouring of divine provision. The blood is the originator of favor and blessings. It transforms curses into blessings, turns setbacks into setups for divine intervention, and converts obstacles into opportunities for God's glory to be manifest. It is the key that unlocks the storehouses of heaven, releasing abundance into the lives of those who understand its power.

The triumph secured by the blood is not a fleeting victory but an enduring state of triumph. It positions the believer in a place of perpetual advantage, seated with Christ in heavenly places, far above all principalities and powers. This triumph is comprehensive, covering every aspect of life—spiritual, physical, emotional, and material. Through the blood, we are more than conquerors, not by our strength or merit, but by the finished work of Christ on the cross.

Yet, the power of the blood extends beyond corporate victory to personal sanctification and purification. It cleanses the conscience from dead works, purifies the heart from unrighteousness, and washes away the stains of sin hindering our communion with God. The blood of Jesus is the detergent of heaven, capable of removing the stubbornest spots and blemishes from our spiritual garments, presenting us faultless before the throne of grace.

As we invoke the blood for personal sanctification, we align ourselves more closely with the divine nature, becoming partakers of God's holiness. This purification process is ongoing, transforming us from glory to glory and conforming us to the image of Christ. The blood not only cleanses us from all unrighteousness but also empowers us to walk in newness of life, resisting temptation and overcoming sin.

The blood of Jesus Christ stands as a wellspring of victory that never dries up with blessing, and transformation. It is God's perfect solution to every problem of humanity, the answer to every question, and the key to unlocking every promise of God. As we continue to plead the blood, invoke its power, and apply its virtues to every area of our lives, we position ourselves for unprecedented breakthroughs and unparalleled manifestations of God's glory.

Let us, therefore, approach the throne of grace with boldness, having our hearts sprinkled from an evil conscience and our bodies washed with pure water. Let us hold fast the profession of our faith without wavering, knowing that He who promised is faithful. And let us never cease to proclaim the power of the blood, for in it lies our assurance of victory, our guarantee of blessing, and our promise of eternal triumph over all the works of darkness.

The blood of Jesus is our eternal testimony, our unshakeable foundation, and our everlasting victory. May we never underestimate its power or neglect its application in our daily walk with God. For in the blood, we find not just deliverance from Satan's schemes, but the very amplification of God's glorious plans for our lives and for all of creation.

Revealing The Glory Of Jesus Through The Blood

For nigh on two decades, the commencement of each morning in my life hath been marked by a great sense of gratitude and a fervent invocation of the precious blood of our Lord Jesus Christ. This practice, far from being a familiar ritual, has become the very bedrock of my spiritual existence, a wellspring of divine power that has sustained me through countless trials and tribulations. I implore thee, dear brethren, to never grow weary or faint-hearted in the calling upon of this most sacred blood, for therein lies a potency beyond mortal comprehension.

Verily, when a believer, through neglect or ignorance, fails to grant the blood of Jesus the opportunity to speak forth its mighty proclamations, they unwittingly deprive themselves of abundance of blessings. For the blood is not merely a instrument of redemption, though that in itself be a wonder beyond measure. Nay, it is the very essence of our salvation, a complete and perfect package that the Greeks of old termed 'Soteria'. This Soteria, this all-encompassing salvation, extends far beyond the mere buying back of our souls from the clutches of sin and death. It is, in truth, a total deliverance that touches every facet of our mortal existence.

Consider the distinction between redemption and salvation. Redemption, in its most basic sense, speaks of a buying back, a reclaiming of that which was lost. What a glorious concept, to be sure, but one that only scratches the surface of what the blood of Christ hath accomplished for us. Salvation, on the other hand, is a far more expansive term, involving not only our redemption but also our healing, our deliverance, our protection, and our ultimate glorification. It is, in essence, the totality of God's restorative work in our lives, made possible through the shedding of His Son's precious blood.

Thus, when we engage the blood to activate our day properly, we are in fact giving this most holy substance the opportunity to speak forth its manifold blessings over every aspect of our lives. Think not that this is a small matter, for the voice of the blood is mighty indeed, capable of silencing the accusations of the enemy and declaring us righteous before the very throne of God. As it is written in the book of Hebrews, "*And to Jesus the mediator of the new covenant, and to the blood of sprinkling, that speaketh better things than that of Abel.*" (Hebrews 12:24, KJV)

The blood of Abel, spilled upon the ground by his brother Cain, cried out to God for vengeance. But the blood of Christ, far more precious and potent, speaks forth everlasting forgiveness, reconciliation, and life. It is a voice that reverberates through the very foundations of the universe, declaring us to be the sons and daughters of the Most High God.

When we invoke the blood of Jesus at the dawn of each new day, we are, in essence, aligning ourselves with this heavenly declaration. We are positioning ourselves to receive the fullness of what Christ has purchased for us through His sacrifice on Calvary. In a genuine sense, we are activating the power of the blood to work on our behalf throughout the hours that lie ahead.

Take it lightly, if thou wilt, the myriad ways in which the blood of Jesus can manifest God's glory in our daily lives. Through its cleansing power, we are made pure and spotless before the Almighty, enabling us to stand in His presence without fear or shame. As the scriptures declare, "*If we walk in the light, as he is in the light, we have fellowship one with another, and the blood of Jesus Christ his Son cleanseth us from all sin.*" (1 John 1:7, KJV)

Moreover, the blood provides supernatural protection against the enemy's wiles. Just as the Israelites of old were shielded from the destroying angel by the blood of the Passover lamb, so too are we covered and protected by the blood of Christ. No weapon formed against us can prosper, and no curse can take hold when we are under the canopy of the blood.

The blood of Jesus grants us access to the very throne room of God. We can approach Him with boldness and confidence, knowing that we have been made acceptable in His sight through the blood of His Son. As it is written, "Having therefore, brethren, boldness to enter into the holiest by the blood of Jesus." (Hebrews 10:19,

KJV)

In light of these truths, how can we not be fervent in our daily invocation of the blood? How can we neglect so great a salvation, a powerful weapon in our spiritual arsenal? Therefore, Let us resolve to give the blood of Jesus its rightful place in our lives, allow it to speak forth its blessings, and manifest the glory of God in tangible, practical ways.

As we do so, we shall find ourselves walking in a new level of victory and authority. We shall see the hand of God moving in our circumstances, opening doors that no man can shut and shutting doors that no man can open. We shall experience a depth of intimacy with the Father that we have previously only dreamed of, all because we have learned to properly engage the blood of Jesus and allow it to speak on our behalf.

Let us, then, approach each new day with a heart full of gratitude and a spirit attuned to the voice of the blood. Let us declare with confidence the efficacy of Christ's sacrifice, knowing that as we do so, we are aligning ourselves with the very purposes of heaven. For it is through the blood that we have been redeemed, through the blood that we are saved, and through the blood that we shall overcome. As it is written in the book of Revelation, "*And they overcame him by the blood of the Lamb, and by the word of their testimony; and they loved not their lives unto the death.*" (Revelation 12:11, KJV)

May the Lord grant us the wisdom and the grace to fully apprehend and appropriate all that He has made available to us through the precious blood of His Son. And may our lives be a living testimony to the power and the glory of that blood, now and forevermore. Amen.

The Blood: The Origin Of New Beginnings

Blood has had special significance as a symbol of sacrifice in the

Old Testament. Take, for example, meat offerings and sacrifices in the Old Testament, where Jews used animals in their religion's forms of worship so as to make a request for forgiveness or even to thank God. The priest would even cut the throat of the animal and collect blood that would be used to sprinkle on the altar. As the Bible says, "*the life of the flesh is in the blood*" (Leviticus 17:11, KJV); thus, by bringing the animal's blood, one was bringing one's life before God.

The shedding of blood is probably best understood in the New Testament narrative through crucifixion, which involved the crucifixion of Jesus Christ. Concerning purification, salvation, and new life, the price for the sin was paid with the life of Jesus Christ crucified on the cross. As Hebrews 9:22 (KJV) says, "*without the shedding of blood is no remission*," which can only be interpreted as forgiveness and reconciling with God needed blood. When Jesus told his disciples at the Last Supper that the wine represented "*my blood of the new testament, which is shed for many for the remission of sins*" (Matthew 26:28, KJV), He tied his coming sacrifice with the bloodshed of the Old Testament rituals, but now as the only real means of purging sin, as well as the Son of God.

That is why, even though the animal sacrifices were stopped with the destruction of the Temple in 70 AD, the rite of the Holy Communion enables Christians to appeal to the saving power of the sacrament and receive Jesus's sacrifice as a sanctifying meal. Wine represents the blood that he spilt to confirm a new covenant with man. As Paul said, "*This cup is the new testament in my blood*" (1 Corinthians 11:25, KJV).

These meanings of the ritual bloodshed include the following personal ones in initiating moral purification and spiritual rebirth: First, it brings remembrance of the evil consequences of sin, therefore helping in repentance. When one thinks of the innocent body and blood being spilled for human sinfulness, it inculcates a sense of the seriousness and destructiveness of sin. As an old hymn states, "My sin, Oh, the blackness of my sin... made the blood flow from his wounds." Acknowledging one's sin to be this deserving results in repentance.

As well, getting into the energy of shed blood makes one tap into the holy archetypal energies of death and renewal. The sight, smell, and touch of blood are associated with life; when there is blood shedding, there is life loss. But it is by means of liquid blood that the woman delivers, and new life is born in her womb. Hence its association with dying and rising, or death and rebirth, which is to say the finality of being and at the same time the possibility of existence. Mobilizing the blood of Christ, one calls into those otherworldly waves of sacrifice and redemption; sin is put to death, and one is born sinless. As the blood-stained water of baptism, so to speak, one comes out cleansed, entities that once were tainted with ill behaviors washed in blood.

Invoking the sacrificial blood powers, the spirit with a divine mission. Jesus died profusely for a noble purpose—this was to restore humanity to divinity. Whenever one uses that consecrated power, committing one's life to the service of Christ's mission, one gets burning passion with which to fan the flame of the cause, accept the values of that noble cause, and spread the rule of the kingdom. Weaknesses and idleness vanish as soon as the person finds his place in something more important than herself. To imitate his sacrifice is to be inflamed by an iron determination to do good.

But in all different rituals of invoking, like the Eucharist or an individual prayer request, Christ's blood is a powerful spiritual change. In Hebrews, the scripture says, *"The blood of Christ... cleanses our conscience."* When naming that blood before God, devotees tap into its holiness as an agent to start with, the process of washing away sin, of being reconciled with Christ and called to live a holy life for his glory. Blood spilt to regain humanity becomes mankind's desire for the spiritual cleansing.

CHAPTER THREE

THE KINGDOM OF GOD AS A REFUGE

The kingdom of God provides salvation, protection, and authority to the people. As Obadiah 1:17 (KJV) says, "But upon mount Zion shall be deliverance, and there shall be holiness; and the house of Jacob shall possess their possessions." This has a promise that in the holy kingdom of God, those who trust in him will be delivered and protected. We do not work our way to kingdom through merit, but rather by believing in the Lord Jesus Christ, one gains salvation. In other words, every citizen of the Kingdom of God must take solace in the safekeeping and stewardship of God.

It expresses the general illumination of the fact that life in this wicked world is full of trouble and fears. We are faced with storms, not just financially but health-wise, and even in our relationships. In contrast, if we recur to the protection of God's kingdom, the storms cannot dominate over us anymore. We have blessed hope and spiritual capital to endure transient suffering. As Paul writes in Philippians 4:13 (KJV), "*I can do all things through Christ which strengtheneth me.*"

We are not only protected but made useful in the inherited kingdom that we have already come into. As 1 Corinthians 2:4 (KJV) reads, "*And my speech and my preaching was not with enticing words of man's wisdom, but in demonstration of the Spirit and of power.*" God's kingdom does not come through human initiatives, but in the way submitted Christians are empowered by the Spirit. When we give ourselves and our skills in the hands of God, he blesses these with divine power. Suddenly what we have, our loaves and fish, is translated and multiplied to feed thousands. Each of the gestures of service that we make here cascades into eternity. Small cracks in what God has fashioned with such care as though vessels of clay will, even in their decay, bring light into this world of darkness.

The refuge and power in the kingdom belong to the divine provision made on grace since the blessed and protected do not contribute anything toward receiving such favor. We can boldly enter His throne room to receive mercy and strength because Jesus paid for our citizenship in His kingdom through His sacrificial death for our sins (Hebrews 4:16). Since we are adopted children of the King, we also have unrestricted permission to be in His strongholds of safety and might. The kingdom resources available to us far surpass earthly riches, for "*But as it is written, Eye hath not seen, nor ear heard, neither have entered into the heart of man, the things which God hath prepared for them that love him.*" (1 Corinthians 2:9, KJV).

As citizens of heaven, we live in this world as ambassadors of Christ's kingdom (2 Corinthians 5:20). While we are temporarily forced to suffer, fight, and suffer more in the enemy's land, we are the epitome of the permanent and eternal kingdom, which shall triumph all. Its territorial borders continue progressing vigorously in human souls as men believe in Christ. One day, the kingdom in all its fullness will descend to earth, "*And the kingdom and dominion, and the greatness of the kingdom under the whole heaven, shall be given to the people of the saints of the highest, whose kingdom is an everlasting kingdom, and all dominions shall serve and obey him.*" (Daniel 7:27, KJV).

Until that great day, we have Christ's spiritual kingdom as our refuge from the peril of sin and as our means of giving out the light of the gospel. The King Himself secures the borders of His kingdom, which cannot be shaken by any weapon the enemy raises against it (Hebrews 12:28). We can confidently build our lives on the unshakable foundation of His kingdom (Luke 6:47–48). As we seek God's kingdom first, making it our greatest priority, we gain security and purpose that earthly kingdoms cannot provide (Matthew 6:33). The perfect world and the vehicle for the kingdom of God are still our permanent shelter and supply of glorious spiritual power.

The Kingdom: A Place Of Safety

God's kingdom provides safety, shelter, and triumph to the people of God even as the world is in chaos. As Psalm 91:1 KJV says, *"He that dwelleth in the secret place of the most High shall abide under the shadow of the Almighty."* God's kingdom is the abode of those who find refuge in Him when facing adversities and challenges. Just as a child has protection and shelter in the arms of that beloved parent, God surrounds his cherished kids with grace and sheer muscle.

This indicates that while there may be storms prevailing over their outside world of sin, the interior of God's kingdom is characterized by peace and safety for the righteous. The God of heaven does not shield his people from suffering, but he will be with them in the suffering. As a loving shepherd, He protects and nurtures her (commonwealth) as a flock. Jesus assures us in John 16:33: *"These things I have spoken unto you, that in me ye might have peace. In the world ye shall have tribulation: but be of good cheer; I have overcome the world."* However, in all situations, God is still in control. Where there are challenges, they don't matter because he has a flawless plan and timing to implement our success.

Also, the kingdom of God is not just a shelter from life's storms but an invulnerable kingdom. What has been created by the hands of men and what is practiced in this world will crumble one day, but the kingdom of God will not. Believers in His kingdom by His grace are more extraordinary than conquerors through Christ Jesus. No opponent is too great, and no temptation is cunning enough to separate the believer from God's divine and powerful shield and guidance. He assures us he will turn everything to work for the benefit of those who will remain loyal to him.

The storms of life come and go, *"but the LORD shall endure forever"* (Psalm 9:7, KJV). Thus, it is possible to expect and believe in God's kingdom. Since we live under God's protection, we are enclosed to nothing that the world may be able to bring upon us. His kingdom sets us free and always succeeds in more than outweighing all the conquests through the One who has loved us.

The identity of being in the kingdom of God is to live under divine protection and dominion. Since we are children of God, we are privileged to draw from the power of the blood of Jesus that was shed for our sin and first death. When we trust in Christ, we are placed under his authority or dominion. This means the fear of the devil or anything dangerous is gone because God is with us and will not allow anything that may harm us to come near.

The blood of Jesus means a new contract that gives many salvation and the restoration of fellowship with the Lord. As the blood of the lambs protected the Israelites whenever the angel of death passed, the blood of Christ protected followers from any traps set by the enemy. Satan has been conquered in Christ, and thus he cannot hold dominion over us for Christ conquered death. In as much as we are in Christ, with His blood metaphorically over us, we are off-bounds to evil spirits.

Not only does Jesus blood work to our benefit or save us, but they even grant us an audience with God. So we can come to Him with that assurance and courageously seek His help since they required it at that time. We have no reason to be afraid because the same Creator and sustainer of the whole universe provides the role of a jealous Father. He said I will never abandon you and will always be with us in the presence of the Lord.

That is how citizens of heaven residing in this world are supposed to walk—in the boldness that comes from the redeemed blood of Christ. We are to be courageous in our testimony, having no knowledge of what could really hurt us. Nothing can ever negate us from God's love, not even death. All that concerns our eternal life is safe, and as much as what concerns our temporal life is in His control. At the heart of it all, depending on the blood means we are free to live in such a way that makes Christ known regardless of threats or persecution. Jesus said that in this world there would be tribulation, but we are to take comfort, for He has conquered the world! This kind of protection given by the blood lets us walk in faith regardless of the storm ahead of us.

Two Ways God Saves His People

God takes pleasure in saving humanity. Basically, there are two ways God saves his children from the trouble of this world. First, he may decide to shift them from areas of hardship or otherwise risky regions. We see examples of this when God closed the door of the ark to shelter Noah and his family from the flood (Genesis 7:16). Similarly, God led Lot and his daughters out of Sodom before destroying it for its wickedness (Genesis 19:15–17). The people of Israel cried when they were oppressed by Pharaoh, and when strong winds blew, God opened the red sea for the people to escape (Exodus 14:10–14). At other times, Jesus withdrew with his disciples to avoid confrontation and dangers (Matthew 14:13, Matthew 15:21). On occasions, God may opt to simply transport His followers out of harm's way, as when Philip was supernaturally taken away after baptizing the Ethiopian eunuch (Acts 8:39-40).

The second method of protection is where God continues to dwell with them during trouble, through the superimposing of His kingdom. Jesus manifested this kingdom reality when asleep onboard a storm-tossed ship, demonstrating God's power to *"speak peace to the storm"* on behalf of those who place their trust in Him (Mark 4:35–41, Psalms 29:10–11). Similarly, when Shadrach, Meshach, and Abednego refused to worship idols, they were not spared from the fiery furnace but went through it unharmed, protected by the Son of God (Daniel 3:25). The early apostles likewise prayed not to be removed from possible dangers they preached among but requested boldness to continue speaking the word of God in the midst of opposition, trusting God's kingdom power (Acts 4:29). Later, Paul and Silas prayed and sang praises while imprisoned, seeing God's power shake open the jail that bound them (Acts 16:25–26).

Sometimes God's people are faced with flood or fire, lions or iron, harassment, famine, or pestilence. But they go through with impunity—by the kingdom of heaven. As the Scriptures promise, *"When thou passest through the waters, I will be with thee; and through the rivers, they shall not overflow thee: when thou walkest through the fire, thou shalt not be burned; neither shall the flame kindle upon thee."* (Mark 8:17). This kingdom shield arises from deep trust in God's sovereign power and protection, which enables His children to *"be strong in the Lord, and in the power of his might."* (Ephesians 6:10 KJV). God's people know the miracle of survival through faith as they confront fear and danger; thus, the glory of God can be seen through.

So God saves through either taking His followers out of the times of trial or protecting them through the victorious kingdom's presence and power. Either way, He demonstrates Himself faithful to sustain and protect His own, fulfilling the promises that *"even though I walk through the darkest valley, I will fear no evil, for you are with me"* (Psalms 23:4) and *'I have said these things to you, that in me you might have peace.' Truly, in this world you will have trouble. But take heart! I have overcome the world"* (John 16:33).

Songs Of Deliverance

You are a hiding place for me; You, Lord, preserve me from trouble, You surround me with songs and shouts of deliverance. Psalm 32:7

God in His infinite wisdom and boundless love, bestows upon His chosen people a most precious gift: the gift of songs. These are not mere melodies to tickle the ear or rhythms to stir the feet, but rather, they are divine compositions, imbued with the very essence of God's manifestation in the lives of His faithful servants. As it is written in the book of Psalms, *"Thou art my hiding place; thou shalt preserve me from trouble; thou shalt compass me about with songs of deliverance."* (Psalm 32:7, KJV) Herein lies a simple but important truth, that the Almighty God not only delivers His people but surrounds them with songs that capture the very essence of that deliverance.

These divinely orchestrated and spiritually resonant celestial harmonies come in a multitude of forms, each serving a unique purpose in the grand tapestry of our spiritual journey. There are songs of power and mighty anthems that shake the very foundations of darkness and declare the omnipotence of our God. These are the battle cries of the faithful, the sonic weapons that cause the walls of Jericho to crumble and the armies of the enemy to flee in terror.

Then there are the songs of deliverance, sweet melodies that testify to the saving grace of our Lord, echoing the sentiments of the Psalmist who declared, *"He brought me up also out of an horrible pit, out of the miry clay, and set my feet upon a rock, and established my goings. And he hath put a new song in my mouth, even praise unto our God: many shall see it, and fear, and shall trust in the LORD."* (Psalm 40:2-3, KJV) These songs are the testimonies of souls snatched from the brink of destruction, now singing praises to their Deliverer.

In the arsenal of divine music, we find songs of protection, spiritual shields that ward off the fiery darts of the wicked one. These are the lullabies of heaven, sung over God's children as they rest in the shadow of the Almighty, secure in the knowledge that *"He shall cover thee with his feathers, and under his wings shalt thou trust: his truth shall be thy shield and buckler."* (Psalm 91:4, KJV)

The bounty of God's provision finds expression in songs of His abundant supply, melodies that remind us of the miraculous multiplication of loaves and fishes, of manna from heaven, and of water from the rock. These are the songs of Jehovah Jireh, our Provider, who *"satisfieth the longing soul, and filleth the hungry soul with goodness."* (Psalm 107:9, KJV)

In the courts of the King, we hear songs of promotion, celestial fanfares that herald the elevation of the humble and the exaltation of the lowly. These are the anthems of Joseph rising from the pit to the palace, of David ascending from the sheepfold to the throne, reminding us that *"He raiseth up the poor out of the dust, and lifteth up the beggar from the dunghill, to set them among princes, and to make them inherit the throne of glory."* (1 Samuel 2:8, KJV)

The heavenly realms resound with ceaseless praise, an eternal symphony of adoration that never falters, never tires. This is the song of the seraphim, crying *"Holy, holy, holy, is the LORD of hosts: the whole earth is full of his glory."* (Isaiah 6:3, KJV) It is the perpetual worship that flows from hearts overwhelmed by the majesty and goodness of our God.

In the journey of faith, we encounter songs of progress, melodic milestones that mark our growth in grace and knowledge of our Lord Jesus Christ. These are the songs of pilgrims pressing toward the mark for the prize of the high calling of God in Christ Jesus, declaring with the Apostle Paul, *"I press toward the mark for the prize of the high calling of God in Christ Jesus."* (Philippians 3:14, KJV)

For those who run the race with patience, there are songs of speed and achievement, divine propeller that propel us forward in our spiritual marathon. These are the anthems of Elijah outrunning Ahab's chariot, of Peter walking on water, reminding us that *"they that wait upon the LORD shall renew their strength; they shall mount up with wings as eagles; they shall run, and not be weary; and they shall walk, and not faint."* (Isaiah 40:31, KJV)

We also hear the triumphant melodies of open doors, songs that declare the removal of barriers and the dawning of new opportunities. These are the victory chants of Paul and Silas, whose praises shook the foundations of their prison and opened every door. They echo the words of Christ to the church in Philadelphia: *"I have set before thee an open door, and no man can shut it."* (Revelation 3:8, KJV)

Indeed, these songs are not mere musical compositions, but rather, they are spiritual keys that unlock the treasuries of heaven. They are a secret to receiving from God, a divine currency that, when invested in our daily lives, yields supernatural returns. For in the economy of God's kingdom, unlike the finite resources of this world, the more we use these songs, the more abundant they become. It is a paradoxical principle that defies earthly logic: in the natural realm, repeated use leads to exhaustion and depletion, but in God's system, consistent activation results in multiplication and increase.

Therefore, let us be diligent in activating these heavenly melodies into our daily lives, for they are investments into our future, seeds of faith sown in the fertile soil of God's promises. As we lift our voices in songs of power, deliverance, protection, provision, promotion, ceaseless praise, progress, speed, achievement, and open doors, we are not merely making music – we are partnering with the divine orchestrator in shaping our destiny. Let every day be filled with these songs, for as we use them, we shall gain more, and our lives shall become a living testament to the transformative power of God's melodious grace.

Living In The Victory Of God's Kingdom

Unlike the kingdoms of this world, which appear and disappear with power and might, the kingdom of God endures. As children of the Lord, we are blessed to already dwell in the Eternal Kingdom in this world.

Jesus announced the arrival of the Kingdom of God in the world. Christ triumphed over sin and death through His life, death on the cross, and His rising from the grave, and He has been exalted King. Even those that believe in Him are enlisted in this kingdom that is eternal in nature.

Thus, as Kingdom citizens, we rule with Jesus; we exercise dominion as co-rulers with the King of Kings. But we do live our lives in a sinful world and have not been delivered from troubles, as we have the power of He who raised up Christ from the dead indwelling us. God will one day finish the work that started in us and brought us to spiritual maturity, to be like His Son. Sometime in the future we will receive it in full when we are presented blameless before the throne of God as those who share His inheritance with Jesus Christ.

It is only in the victory of this kingdom that a believer's view of every fight changes as a result of God's sovereignty. No longer have we become vulnerable to attacks of the enemy, but now we possess divine strength to withstand. When sickness, financial pressure, broken relationships, or other tests come, we know that all things work together for good for those who love the Lord. For as we consider this present time, our momentary light afflictions are producing for us an eternal weight of glory beyond comparison.

In Kingdom citizenship, devotion is due to God and His causes. Even if we are in the world, we don't see war as merely being carnal, and our fight is not of the flesh. Our weapons are not carnal but instead divine force and Kingdom strategy to dismantle various systems of the world. We engage in the battle already, knowing that we have already won through the blood of Christ.

God wants us to work in transforming this world so that it conforms to his kingdom. They ask us His ambassadors to govern with the rule and reign of Jesus through the ministry of actualization, speaking the truth in love, acts of power, and true gospel. Sometime in the future every knee will bow to King Jesus, which is rather comforting to think about. Until then, we provide God's Kingdom illumination where darkness prevails, and we combat evil forces while confidently occupying Kingdom territory.

We can sleep tight with the knowledge that we belong to an immoveable kingdom. These are the war cries and roaring lions as we live each day in the bosom of our triumphant King, which transforms our thinking and our behavior by the virtues of the Kingdom until we overcome every adversary in the strength of His might. Thus, we have kingdom breakthrough in every sphere of our lives when we trudge ourselves to His Lordship all the way. Yet while the struggle continues for us in the present age while we wait for the coming of Christ, we have already gotten victory through Him.

CHAPTER FOUR

THE WORD OF GOD – YOUR GUIDE TO VICTORY

The word of God is a lamp unto the believer's feet and a defense to all those who put their trust in Him. As Hebrews 4:12 states, "For the word of God is quick, and powerful, and sharper than any two-edged sword, piercing even to the dividing asunder of soul and spirit, and of the joints and marrow, and is a discerner of the thoughts and intents of the heart." The word of God speaks to the depths of our hearts and points out our very selves, negating and teaching. When one is in proper standing with the word of God, it becomes mightily at work in influencing one's thoughts, emotions, and behavior.

As the prophet Isaiah stated, "*So shall my word be that goeth forth out of my mouth: it shall not return unto me void, but it shall accomplish that which I please, and it shall prosper in the thing whereto I sent it.*" (Isaiah 55:11, KJV). The word of God never fails in its intended goal—bringing forth fruit from our lives through the agency of the Holy Spirit. Thus, as the scriptures are engaged in—studying, meditating upon, and obeying—they transform us, and we become more Christlike. Of course, they enlighten us on the record as a reflection of 'God's thoughts, will, and ways, as you pointed out. It restores our hearts to think God's thoughts, recalibrates our hearts to want His perfect will, and transforms our actions to do His righteous ones.

That sounds great, and the word will never be powerless. This means that when people focus on negative thoughts or experiences, they will continue to be affected. But the Scripture says that when we are inundated with God's strong message, it transforms and cleanses us from the dark influences over time. Romans 12:2 shows how the change of mind that comes from the word of God removes our tendency toward conformity to the world: "*And be not conformed to this world: but be ye transformed by the renewing of your mind, that ye may prove what that good, and acceptable, and perfect, will of God is.*" When turning to the Scripture, we commit our hearts to it, and the Holy Spirit uses it to purify our thoughts and works to manifest God's will for our sanctification.

The word of God serves as a lamp to guide us through life's darkness (Psalm 119:105). It also provides the right living instruction and directs to the Savior's presence. Because the mind is being renewed by the Word of God, the Holy Spirit now assists in sanctifying every aspect of our lives. This includes everything in our lives: our words, behavior, job, the work that we do in the church and in the community, and even in our relationships. It means the more the Word of God infuses into our lives, the more our mental processes, speech, and deeds will conform to the will of God's kingdom.

The word of the Lord proves true (2 Samuel 7:28). In creating our lives on it, we get to establish stability and strength to endure any adversity. The word of God speaks to us in times of trouble, soothing and encouraging us to rise up and keep on. The scriptures guide us in helping us overcome our suffering and understand things in light of eternity. They give unyielding assurance of God's keeping His word of faith. The word of God being filled by the spirit turns around everything to be victorious. It equips us to minister to others also walking through deep waters and flames of fire (Isaiah 43:2).

If our hearts are given over to the study and application of scripture, it produces much good in and through us through the agency of the Holy Spirit. I am more in tune with Jesus in my head and heart, and we live more victoriously. The people discover Jesus in and through us, to the glory of God. The word of God holds good promises in guiding as well as endowing spiritual strength to those who trust in it. It raises up people for His purposes in those who are being saved. O happy multitude, may we, through believing, build our lives upon this sure foundation every day.

The Word As A Power Source

The word of God as disclosed in the Bible is full of power. Thus Scripture read, studied, and applied becomes a directing force in our thought, belief, and behavior. Lastly, in its broadest sense, the word of God is used to bring people closer to Him and conform them to His will.

The Bible teaches that God's plans for each person are often mysterious or unseen to us. Jeremiah 29:11 KJV, *"For I know the thoughts that I think toward you, saith the LORD, thoughts of peace, and not of evil, to give you an expected end."* The best way for us to learn of His vision is through reading the Scriptures. When we think through scriptures, God throws light upon them and unveils new aspects of our spirit that could have never occurred to us. We start developing knowledge of the special blessing and callings that await us up in Heaven.

This revelation equally comes with specific directions from God of how to transition into our divine purposes. Scripture says in Isaiah 30:21 KJV, *"And thine ears shall hear a word behind thee, saying, This is the way, walk ye in it, when ye turn to the right hand, and when ye turn to the left."* whether to the right or to the left. Prosperity, according to Scripture, is God's hand clearing up our ways by revealing the actions we should take, people we should meet, skills we should cultivate and our manner of going on in the journey of life. His word then leads us to those areas of common ministry, meaningful employment and intrinsic blessing.

But as we seek His will with the submission of our hearts, then we are enabled to obtain the full measure of our spiritual blessings. In it we obtain the grace, enabling, and favor that are necessary for achieving our greatest kingdom destinies. Scripture provides us with knowledge, power, delight and all else that is necessary for holy, happy living. The Psalmist declares in Psalm 119:105 KJV, "Your word is a lamp to my feet, And a light to my path." The word provides illumination on the way so that people can travel it with explicitness, assurance as well as high anticipation.

Therefore, the Scripture is God's word, providing the permanent and crucial power source for life. Each of these areas implies the belief and practice of the Bible, as revelation liberates one's spiritual essence as well as destiny. Some of what the apostle is talking about becomes clear to us, while before it was obscure, and gives us insight as to what God's plan is. We also receive up-to-date instruction on what to do in order to release the blessings that are lined up for us. The word of God also guides our lives and as we live out our callings that God has given us we are unstuck, our paths made clear and we become wiser and stronger in our faith. Scripture gives us a link to the Spirit and to the reality of the now and the not yet of the age to come.

Aligning With God's Will

Remaining in the will of God is the way to live a victorious, blessed, and fulfilling life as a Christian. As believers, when we hear the word of God and surrender to His lordship, we are prepared for the best that's in store for us. As Romans 12:2 (KJV), "And be not conformed to this world: but be ye transformed by the renewing of your mind, that ye may prove what is that good, and acceptable, and perfect, will of God." The heart, or mind, must be renewed with the truth of Scripture before one can truly find God's will and follow it as guided by the Father.

What does it imply to be in the right spirit or obedience to God's plan? At its core level, it presupposes faith in His nature, will, and dealings as being righteous, benign, and accurate. It means laying down our plans and expectations of what He wants us to accomplish in the scriptures. It seems to be pursuing holiness, loving our neighbors, using our talents to strengthen the body of Christ, doing our duties as we should, and walking in godly wisdom with the unbelievers. Ephesians 5:15-17 (KJV) urges, "*See then that ye walk circumspectly, not as fools, but as wise, Redeeming the time, because the days are evil. Wherefore be ye not unwise, but understanding what the will of the Lord is.*" Sin is the opposite of the way that is pleasing to God and results in suffering and death when followed.

There is no comparison of all the rewards and success achieved in adhering to the Lord's will as opposed to our own desires. It saves much grief and sorrow when one accepts the Lord's way as the last word. He leads us to what will finally be fulfilled rather than propelling us into a cycle of pursuing things to nowhere. When we cry to Him for guidance and read the Word, we have the director's cut on the best way to go about our lives. When we follow His instructions, even though the throes of adversity, He also assures His presence as a supplier of power and encouragement when we are persecuted for doing the right things. The fruit of the Holy Spirit—love, joy, peace, forbearance, kindness, etc.—are all borne out of a yielding spirit. Therefore, by focusing our faith on Jesus as an active living faith, He turns the story of one's life from just ordinary into something extraordinary than one can ever conceive.

Thus, obedience to God's will also involves the virtues of humility, courage, and perseverance. It means accepting that we are not omniscient and our approach, our methods, are not the best there is. It requires patience when we not only fail to see what He is doing but also do not know how our obedience will pay off. To die is to give up the self, or, in other words, the warfare in the soul continues as our wills fight His. The world will not approve the radical lifestyle of putting Christ first in our lives. There are expenses incurred—which are often prohibitive—in terms of social, economic, and organizing losses, sufferings, and sacrifices. Jesus himself affirmed this, saying in Matthew 16:24 (KJV), "Whoever wants to become a disciple of Mine must deny himself and take up his cross and follow me." But the gain can never be compared to the loss. Be happy with Jesus, bear fruit that shall never fade away, and be welcomed home by the Lord with the words, "Well done, thou good and faithful servant."

For us as believers, it means to embrace the fact that the way forward has been made available by redeeming grace. When we fall or when there is a misstep, there is forgiveness and mercy that will follow. Instead of punishment for failure, we get a Father who welcomes us with open arms, redeems, and encourages us. Our security does not even lay in the power and the security forces; it lays in who He is. When we are not too sure, He is still sure of His love and plans towards us. Being His children, believing that we are called and empowered by the Holy Spirit, we don't have to be afraid to take steps by faith to be obedient. The deeper we are in fellowship with God, the more our hearts do with the will of God, or vice versa. His word and spirit assure us that every noble cause carried out in obedience to the gospel will achieve its intended purpose. Living according to God's plan brings blessings, as everything He plans always happens. The invitation lies now for an overflowing existence painted by destiny, significance, productiveness, and fellowship with Him in the process of returning.

Obedience Unlocks Blessings

The blessing if you obey the commandments of the Lord your God which I command you this day" (Deuteronomy 11:27) AMP

God teaches us how we should live in order to lead a healthy and blessed life. When we do as He says, something good always results. We get good things from Him.

What does it mean to obey God? It means obeying what He would have us to do according to the scriptures. For instance, God told the people that they should love their neighbors. So, when we love others, that is when we show some kind of act in the way that God wants us to. Only if one obeys what the Lord is saying can they explain why positive blessings are received.

All that the Lord wants to do is pour blessings on His children. As a loving Father, He wants the very best for us and has great plans prepared (Jeremiah 29:11). But it is necessary to follow God's word if one wants to receive all the fullness of his blessings. The reward for those who will pay attention to God's voice and follow what he says is a huge return.

What does it mean to be obedient? Webster's dictionary defines the word obedience as "conformity to an order or a request or to a law." For those pursuing to follow Christ as Christians, simply and most specifically, this entails listening to the Word of God and subsequently correspondingly our demeanor, thoughts, and behaviors to what the Word of God teaches us. Walking in genuine faith is demonstrated through our works (James 2:17). God is pleased when His children obey Him, just as any parent finds joy in their child's willing obedience (1 Samuel 15:22).

Piety is obedience in response to an orderly trust in God. Given that our heavenly Father is perfect, holy, all-knowing, and all-powerful, He understands what is best for us at any given time much better than we do. If we listen to what He has to say and follow it, we will surely be rewarded for doing so. But if we choose the world's way as our way of doing things, it will only be a way of pain and destruction. We must daily choose whether we will be led by the Spirit of God or our feeble human understanding

(Proverbs 3:5–6).

What are some of the beautiful blessings that are open only to the obedient? God promises to meet all of our needs (Philippians 4). Edwards further states that they help grant us perfect peace (Isaiah 26:3), success (Joshua 1:8), and joy (John 15:10-11). He further assures us that obedience will lead to blessings being poured out so abundantly that there will not be room to receive them all (Malachi 3:10)! Of course, the greatest blessing is getting to know Him more closely each day in the process of becoming. As we often establish intimacy with another person through the time spent together, we relate to God through the acts of following His instructions.

However, the spiritual rewards that come as a result of obedience are not only the blessings in this life. They extend to all eternity. Jesus said if we love Him by keeping His commands, He and the Father will come and make Their home with us (John 14:23). Is there any greater privilege than living in the blessed presence of the Lord in a perfect fellowship beyond the ages? Faithful obedience leads ultimately to the supreme blessing and reward of hearing "Well done, good and faithful servant" as we enter our eternal heavenly home (Matthew 25:23).

As God always rewards the obedient, only misery results from the deliberate walking in disobedience. That is in a very painful way evident, especially by the examples of Adam and Eve and the Israelites wandering in the desert. When Adam and Eve disobeyed God's sole instruction that was to avoid eating from the forbidden tree in the Garden of Eden, all sorts of miseries ranging from sin, sickness, and suffering overwhelmed them and all generations to come (Genesis 3). Similarly, Moses' people who complained and revolted against the Lord in the wilderness endured 40 years of wandering until every unbelieving generation of the "wondering" generation dropped dead and never got to set foot in the promised land of milk and honey (Numbers 14).

Just as a parent disciplines the children they love (Hebrews 12:6), the Lord will discipline us so that when we are rebellious, He will correct us and bring us back to the right path. Our loving Father wants nothing more than for us to walk in obedience so we can receive His good and perfect gifts (James 1:17). These are blessings He promises, and thus they are beyond measure, magnificent, and everlasting. As King David proclaimed, "No good thing does He withhold from those who walk uprightly" (Psalm 84:11).

May we have eyes to see the love of the Father, who placed His sheep in the hands of the Good Shepherd. If we follow Him in obedience, accepting His Word as our guide, we shall discover we are partakers of a great treasure laid away from the foundation of the age. Oh, bring the whole reasoning of creation to the tests and see that the Lord is good. Blessed is the man who takes refuge in him!" (Psalm 34:8 ESV).

The Eternal Power Of God's Word

The word of God is strong and enduring. The Bible has literally given mankind many lessons that can still be imparted to us till this generation, despite the thousands of years.

We learn how God expects man to live through stories, commandments, poetry, and letters. These writings, therefore, teach the people of God how to make the right decisions in life. There may be changes in the world, but people remain the same. The same sins, relational issues, questions, and problems in life plague us today as ever since the early days. For this reason, advice and commands in the Bible remain accountable in the current world. Ideals concerning what people do and who they are do not change.

For instance, the Ten Commandments that God provided to Moses as narrated in the book of Exodus of the Bible are against deeds such as stealing or murder and giving false testimony or covetousness. These are actually problems that individuals have to face in the present generation! For all that as a race we undergo metamorphoses in matters of culture and etiquette, basic morality remains the same. What was described as sinful in the past is still considered wrongdoing. This shows that the knowledge of God's commands is indeed profound.

Moreover, preaching the word of God on matters such as forgiveness, being kind to others, marriage, and parenting are still an issue of concern today. Take Jesus's words in Matthew 7:12 KJV, *"Therefore all things whatsoever ye would that men should do to you, do ye even so to them: for this is the law and the prophets."* This powerful and yet basic tenet supports loving your neighbors across time, regardless of generation. It advises on how human beings should be relating to each other regardless of the transformations in society over the centuries.

The Bible also provides good comfort and brings promising promise. When one reads promises from the almighty, then one knows that everything is in order, even when the world itself is in a state of confusion. Psalm 46:1 This admits it: *"God is our refuge and strength, a very present help in trouble."* How comforting are these words to those who trust today when they find themselves in the furnace?!

Also, there is constancy presented with God and Christ's love, as well as the provision for securing the future that is presented through scripture. Jesus declares in John 13:34, *"This is My commandment, that you love one another as I have loved you."* John 3:16 (KJV) Consider how society may change if people's God the Father and Jesus the Son's instructions were strictly adhered to and people loved others as Christ loved them; that is selfless love.

The Bible looks forward to the coming of eternal life with classic pictures of heaven. They are moving signs, which create hope that something sweet is waiting for us in the sky and that all trials of human life are worth it. That is why keeping these prophetic scriptures as more of a guide reminds Christians that there is more to look forward to in the future if they obey God.

All in all, despite technological advances in the world, human hearts remain the same. Man continues to crave ethical leadership, solace during hard times, affection, and hope. The Bible provides all this and many more with solutions and proclamations having no genetic limitations. The stories, historical facts, precepts, guidance, and promises in the divine scriptures do not lose their bearings or cease to be authoritative for man's life of yesterday, today, and tomorrow. That is why the impact of the Bible is felt till today; it originated from the first timeless being—God Himself. His living Word still works creatively and is able to men unto all generations by the Spirit's enlightenment.

CHAPTER FIVE

WITNESSING
THE POWER OF
THE BLOOD

The precious blood of Jesus Christ is more potent than the blood bulls and goats offered in sacrifices by the priests in the Old Testament. As Christians, we believe and speak it in our daily lives and invoke its supernatural power to heal, deliver, and shield.

The Bible says in 1 Peter 1:18-19 (KJV): "Forasmuch as ye know that ye were not redeemed with corruptible things, as silver and gold, from your vain conversation received by tradition from your fathers; But with the precious blood of Christ, as of a lamb without blemish and without spot." The Lord Jesus Christ gave His precious blood in order to redeem our souls. We are bought with the precious blood of the Lamb of God and not by the purchase of silver. This blood is eternal; its potency does not wane.

Every Christian has a chance to use the blood of Jesus daily in their lives, families, and anything that concerns us. When we do, it creates a wall that the enemy cannot penetrate. The blood helps to shield us from demonic attacks, oppression, affliction, and any other thing that is against our lives and sent by the devils. It protects our physical self, our mental health, and our feelings.

Revelation 12:11 (KJV) states it this way: "And they overcame him by the blood of the Lamb and by the word of their testimony.' Through our mouths as we confess the power of the blood, make the devil a loser. The blood disarms the weapons and gives a final win to the child of God.

Besides, the blood signifies a safety net over the covenant blessings that God has promised to bestow on us as His children. Healing, provision, protection, freedom from sin—regeneration through Christ welcomes God's multi-faceted favor and mercy. When therefore we say, 'The blood of Jesus Christ be upon me', or 'Let the blood of Jesus Christ be my witness', it is this divine seal that is releasing these spiritual blessings. In faith, we appropriate all that Jesus' death has provided us. The highest aspect of blood is that the blood is life. Scripture tells us that life is in the blood (Leviticus 17:11). The blood of Jesus Christ, the only sinless one, is blood brimming with undying, eternal life! It transfuses us with the vitality of Christ Himself, making us partakers of His divine nature (2 Peter 1:2). The blood of Jesus is always dealing with eternity. When we apply it in faith, it cleanses our conscience and empowers us to serve God wholeheartedly here and now (Hebrews 9:14), whereby He hath obtained an eternal inheritance for us, which is the glory of being in his everlasting kingdom.

For the blood, what exciting secrets and graces are revealed by it! In the color 'crimson,' we behold the beauty of what Christ has done through His propitiatory act. Indeed, by faith, when we take hold of this spiritual weapon—this emerald river that originates from the mercy seat—the heavens. Having done so, the gates are opened for the miraculous, the breakthroughs, and the overwhelming change across our lives. Even in this little amount of blood, there is great power! Beholding these wonders, unbelievers make me exclaim together with Paul, "Oh God! How deep are your wisdom and knowledge?" (Romans 11:33). According to the efficacy of the blood of the Lamb indeed applied, the majesty of the Almighty opens on the unveiling.

As the blood of Christ was spilled on the cross two thousand years ago, people continue to be saved and made new by the power of that blood. After Jesus died, the veil in the temple was ripped from top to bottom, meaning that there was now a direct way to God because of Jesus's death. As in Hebrews 10:19-20 KJV it is written, *"Having therefore, brethren, boldness to enter into the holiest by the blood of Jesus, By a new and living way, which he hath consecrated for us, through the veil, that is to say, his flesh."*

Additionally, Christ's blood provides eternal redemption (Hebrews 9:12 KJV, *"Neither by the blood of goats and calves, but by his blood he entered in once into the holy place, having obtained eternal redemption for us."*

Its power is eternal, and when received by faith, believers become recipients of all the spiritual blessings arising out of Calvary's once-for-all offering. From the moment of justification, through sanctification, up to and including glorification—all is provided to those rescued by the blood of the Lamb.

This power they have derived from the blood of the Lamb, as the famous hymn of the same title sings. It means that through prayer in Jesus' name and invoking that sort of power, Christians can overcome sins, diseases, demons, and other evils. As Ephesians 1:7 says, "In whom we have redemption through his blood, the forgiveness of sins, according to the riches of his grace." The blood bestows unmerited favors that enable believers to live victorious everyday lives. While salvation is received once in the same manner—by faith—apart from works in Christ's completed work, continued grace is sought through the blood of Christ—the sign of the eternal covenant between God and man. The power of its working continues to perform miracles even today.

The Blood And The Spirit

The Holy Spirit is actively involved in the life of any believer by infusing His presence, voice, and power. After Jesus ascended to heaven, He sent the Holy Spirit to continue His work on earth (John 14:16–17). The Spirit is sent to be Christ's sponsor—to make His presence known, to speak His messages, and to act in the same manner as He does.

The Holy Spirit's presence with us is Jesus physically represented.

The organic part of the Spirit's ministry is therefore to constantly and very tangibly bring the presence of Jesus into the life of a Christian. Although physically Jesus sits at the Father's right hand in heaven (Romans 8:34), and, in a spiritual but truly meaningful way, the Spirit begets the Christians as their presence becomes His dwelling. As Jesus promised His disciples, "I will not leave you comfortless; *And I will come to thee*" (John 14:18 KJV). This He had done through sending the counselor—the Holy Spirit—to abide in us and fellowship with them intimately (John 14:16–17).

The presence of Christ is perceived, and faith is realized based on the Spirit. The apostle Paul describes followers of Jesus as "the temple of the living God" because "*the Spirit of God dwelleth in you*" (2 Corinthians 6:16 KJV). One of the Spirit's leading roles is to take the things of Christ and reveal them to believers (John 16:13–15). As such, 'the spirit of Jesus Christ dwelleth in thee' entails the Christian experiencing 'the Spirit of Jesus'—that's, a comforting, leading, and communion-giving Spirit.

When bringing Jesus voice, the Spirit conveys certain messages to the believers from Christ Himself. In one way He does this, and that is by enlightening the words of the Scripture. David prophesied of this work of the Spirit, saying, "*The voice of the LORD is powerful; the voice of the LORD is full of majesty. The voice of the LORD breaketh the cedars; yea, the LORD breaketh the cedars of Lebanon.*" (Psalm 29:4-5 KJV). Though at one time God's voice "shook the earth" from Mount Sinai during the Exodus, now through the Holy Spirit the voice of His rings in our hearts as it applies and reveals the truths of the Savior.

The Spirit also represents the directions of Christ in terms of innate impulses and inner voice in decision-making processes of life. Isaiah 30:21 and said to them, *"And thine ears shall hear a word behind thee, saying, This is the way, walk ye in it, when ye turn to the right hand, and when ye turn to the left."* (NKJV). This inner voice is a direct call of God's Spirit to give direction so specific and unique that it is as if Jesus is guiding you to choose between two roads.

Jesus said of the Spirit, *"He will guide you into all truth...and He will tell you things to come"* (John 16:13 NKJV). Remaining attentive to such directions helps the Christian faithful to always hear and respond to the soft voice of Christ.

The last method through which the Spirit makes Christ present is revealing that He is at work through the members of the body, confirming the reality of the miracles of Christ. Just before ascending, Jesus promised, *"But ye shall receive power, after that the Holy Ghost is come upon you."* (Acts 1:8 KJV). That seen that day was just a sample of the continuous work of the Spirit that is continually distributing more spiritual gifts and divine power to the church. Paul described it as being *"strengthened with might by His Spirit in the inner man"* (Ephesians 3:16 KJV). Every work of salvation—signs and wonders, triumph over sin, vocal presentation of the gospel—stems from the operation of the Spirit of Christ within His body.

This is why Paul could confidently declare, *"I can do all things through Christ who strengthens me"* (Philippians 4:13 NKJV), and the spirit of the Lord came into him with an omnipotent resource of Jesus. Through God's power at work within us (1 Corinthians 12:(4-6)), the Spirit is what allows believers to go on completing the miracles of Jesus and the expansion of His kingdom (John 14:12). When followers surrender themselves to the control of the Spirit and the power to direct them, Jesus' supernatural power is evident.

The Holy Spirit has an unusual ministry of leading the believers to Christ's presence, to hear His voice, and to unleash His power on earth. He dwells within as a pledge guaranteeing their glorious future hope (Ephesians 1:13–14), simultaneously making the Jesus life reality present here and now. This means that the Spirit's ministry provides for the Christians constant access to the fellowship with, the direction by, the enablement of, and the empowerment by their reigning Savior. As Paul summarizes, by the Spirit, God seeks to fill believers "with all the fullness of God" (Ephesians 3:19 KJV), allowing all of the heavenly blessings and every aspect of the full, living, and powerful life of Jesus Christ to be at home in and enrich the church.

The Three Witnesses On Earth

The three witnesses on earth—water, blood, and spirit—are crucial in Christianity. All three bear witness to some fundamental realities about God, human sin, human salvation, and the new life now available through union with the risen Christ.

The public mainly associates water with ideas of washing and cleaning; hence, the Jews used water to signify a rebirth. Valid baptism refers to the washing of the body by water and the clean birth of the soul by the power of the Holy Spirit. As 1 John 5:8 says, "*And there are three that bear witness in earth, the Spirit, the water, and the blood: and these three agree in one.*" The water speaks of the redemption done by God in our hearts. In the Old Covenant, people used a lot of washing rituals and many cleansings with water. These pointed ahead to the spiritual cleansing and regeneration that Christ was to provide. When Jesus came into the world to begin the ministry, He was baptized in the Jordan River by John the Baptist. This is due to Jesus identifying with sinners and being ready to bear the world's sins. Those who trust their souls to Christ are submerged into the death and life of Christ. The element of water of baptism is that it denotes a new life in him.

The blood of Jesus Christ that he shed on the cross is yet another witness on earth. As it says in Hebrews 9:22 (KJV), *"And almost all things are by the law purged with blood; and without shedding of blood is no remission."* The blood suffers the consequence of our sins, which satisfies God's anger against us. During the time of the judgment in the Passover, the bloodshed protected the Israelites from God's wrath; the wrath passed over them. This pointed to Jesus, the ultimate Passover Lamb, whose shed blood avails for the remission of sin and who, by His blood protection, can shield from future judgment. The blood procured for the sinners' ransom justifies us in the sight of God. Jesus said at the Last Supper that His blood was *"shed for many for the remission of sins"* (Matthew 26:28). He and his blood cry out today, proclaiming that Jesus died once for all the sins of the world.

The Holy Spirit Himself witnesses on earth concerning the operations of God in the heart of man. Jesus told His disciples that when the Spirit came, *"He will testify of Me"* (John 15:26). The Spirit inspired the writing of Scripture to testify about Jesus (John 16:13–15). And the Spirit convicts people's hearts of sin, righteousness, and judgment—drawing them to trust Christ (John 16:8–11). So far as the acts of the gospel are concerned, every saved man will receive the operation of the new birth and the Holy Spirit. As Paul says in Romans 8:16 KJV, *"The Spirit itself beareth witness with our spirit, that we are the children of God."* Salvation sanctifies us so that we are to become like Christ, and then the Spirit bestows this adopted son/daughter status.

All these three witnesses testify that Jesus Christ is the world's Savior. The water typifies the putting away of sin; the blood typifies the putting away of sin's penalty; and the Spirit typifies the creation of a new spiritual life through faith in Christ. Combined, they declare the totality of the work of redemption that God has done for us. Believing the water, the blood, and the Spirit brings us to the God-given assurance, safety, peace, and happiness within the Christian life.

Revealing The True Jesus

The blood of Jesus Christ is the medium through which power from above is employed to change lives to reflect the glory of the Son. When we place our faith and trust in Christ's shed blood, relying wholly on its atoning efficacy, we become partakers of His divine nature (2 Peter 1:2).

Using prayer and faith while administering the blood, the Holy Spirit seals us, transforming our character and behavior to be more like Christ's. "But we all, with open face beholding as in a glass the glory of the Lord, are changed into the same image from glory to glory, even as by the Spirit of the Lord." (2 Corinthians 3:18, KJV).

This inner change becomes evident in an outward process, where we become instruments of Jesus. We begin to love others as Christ loves; we begin to seek lost individuals, embrace sinful men, and forgive sinful men through the preaching of salvation. In that perfect love, we start to love through the spiritual feeling of the power that brought Jesus back to life. The divinity of Christ is manifested as His life and power flow through sanctified vessels baptized with the blood of the Savior.

Where there was sin, we see virtue; where there was sinfulness, we see saintliness after the Lord, who willingly gave up His own life. Where once hostility prevailed, there blooms now love and charity of Christ. Where there were once the cruel constraints of sin to confine and restrict the one to whom they were bound, there is now the sweet liberty that comes with the blood and the life that makes prisoners out of bonds. As blood washes all the spots, we display the image of God's holy and righteous Son.

This is all not of our doing but out of surrender to the transforming work of the Holy Spirit and in pleading for the blood of Jesus Christ daily. It is not what we suffer or what we suffer for that saves us; it is the holy, precious blood of Jesus, shed for us, which reconciles us to God through faith alone. The lyrics of one of the older hymns would best answer the question, "What can wash away my sins?" And this, the blood of Jesus saved me."

The blood turns our gaze to the cross, where the God-sent Lamb of God offered up divine blood as the propitiation for our sins. The honest Jesus does not rest in garments of ecclesiastical dead works, which negate this power of change. The honest Jesus having announced on the Cross, *"It is finished,"* there was no further task for man to perform but to appropriate in faith the completed work of Christ.

This Jesus now dwells in each believer through the agency of the Holy Spirit, progressively transforming and sanctifying us so that every area of our lives is subject to His lordship. The renewal is effected by the blood carried on by the heart of the new creature; of course, the believer bears an inevitable tendency to go out in the lines of righteousness. As the spirit brings Christ into our minds and hearts, we become smaller so He may become more outstanding. Thus, others come face to face with Jesus Christ as their Savior through a church where Jesus has been rendered pure and white through the shed blood of the Lamb.

When people look at us through the lens of lives surrendered to the saving grace of the Savior, they see the outlived love of a crucified Lord. The praying, weeping Savior who broke the dawn nights in prayer comes out through redeemed sinners with His heart for the lost generation. It is Christ who came to seek out the one lost sheep, and He binds wandering souls to Himself through those who appeal to his blood. His divinity is not crowned with the input of the makeup of man, so this is why the Jesus in me, totally surrendered to His complete lordship, is revealed best.

This is the power of the blood: to wash out all sin and the garment of sinful fleshliness that obscures the actual image of Christ in His bride. Each, as he partakes while using the blood in surrender and in faith and in partaking the cup the savior drank, we become living Holy of Holies temples' where the glory of God may dwell without check. Only then shall the world behold the faithful Jesus when He shall appear through His bride made ready through the crimson flood from heaven.

The Supernatural Confidence From The Blood

Believers gain authority and power through His precious blood shed for them through the crucifixion of Jesus Christ. It is such confidence in eternal redemption that comes with the cross that makes us confront evil, proclaim freedom, and extend the kingdom of God.

We're not fighting with the weapons of this world, which are flesh and blood, against powers and principalities that are demonic and Gnostics. Instead, we live in miraculous power deriving from the Easter victory accomplished at the cross. Jesus said, *"Behold, I give unto you power to tread on serpents and scorpions, and over all the power of the enemy, and nothing shall by any means hurt you"* (Luke 10:19, KJV). The blood of Jesus helps us to stand against and deliver ourselves from Satan or demonic control.

Moreover, we are in a divine position to challenge systems of sin and injustice. By embracing the crucified and resurrected Jesus, we are empowered to declare the truth, rebuke the evil, stand for justice, and liberate people from the cycle of their worst sins. The blood of the Lamb emboldens us to proclaim liberty to the oppressed, just as our Savior declared His messianic mission *"to preach deliverance to the captives"* (Luke 4:18, KJV).

When wielding the sword of the Spirit in praying for deliverance or for spiritual outworkings, instead of the troll of fear, the believers can wield clerical courage, knowing that they are co-creators with God and the forces of the devil are no match to the blood of Jesus. The apostle Paul states, "If God is for us, who can be against us?" (Romans 8:31, KJV). John revealed that He who is in the us is more significant than He in the world. No opponent is able to resist or reverse what Christ has done—power of the cross. Hence, it is our commitment to forward His kingdom without any compromise.

This spiritual confidence does not come from within us, but it comes from the believer trusting in Jesus's completed work. His propitiatory action provides us with spiritual life, power, and victory. We fought as it were with divine ordinance and might because man's own resources are insufficient to bring down bastions that have been years in the making.

The power of Calvary produces confidence in the hearts of men and women, so they become soldiers for God's glory. Without despairing for one moment that the blood is efficacious for the everlasting, we pay no attention to the devil but march straight to the gates of hell. Eager at a personal price by Jesus' love, we cannot but continue to preach and apply His gospel until He prevails in victory.

We treat this fallen world with dignity and state confidently, as those bought with the blood of Christ, that we have glorious treasures to declare the one who has saved us from darkness. This supernatural confidence that Jesus' blood never loses its power stirs us to go out and to shout redemption to the unsaved and liberty to the captives. His love compels us onward.

CHAPTER SIX

THE HAND OF GOD UPON YOU

When I use the phrase "hand of God," I mean that the Lord is directing or defending us. God's endowments signify supernatural anointing, preferential treatment, enabler, and assistance to enable the fulfillment of additional purposes in His creation's life.

The whole of scripture reveals how God's hand strengthens his people. In the story of Nehemiah rebuilding the walls of Jerusalem, Nehemiah testifies that it was through God's gracious help and favor that allowed him to succeed, saying, "According to the good hand of my God upon me" (Nehemiah 2:8, KJV). This goes to prove that with God's help, one is able to achieve the impossible on earth by sheer strength.

God's hand upon us brings strength through deliverance from harm and adversity. Another way whereby God upholds us in strength is through the delivery we receive from harm and adversity. Isaiah 41:10 (KJV) It says, "Fear thou not; for I am with thee: be not dismayed; for I am thy God: I will strengthen thee; yea, I will help thee; yea, I will uphold thee with the right hand of my righteousness." This can be used to explain how the power of his right is security and a sounding board in times that we feel threatened by fear or trouble. It embraces the phrase, which says His hand is our protecting power and help in distress.

More specifically, having the hand of God upon your life means experiencing some key manifestations of His power and blessings:

- *Calling:* God directs you towards where He wants you to be for life, purpose, and direction. You get knowledge and understanding of which roads to take and which openings to seize. Psalms 32:8 (KJV) states, "I will instruct thee and teach thee in the way which thou shalt go: I will guide thee with mine eye." Propriety works in your favor even when the whole world appears to be against you. This is because God is on your side. He felt doors opening, of which no man can shut. You have moments of strange curtesy and assistance. As Genesis 39:2 KJV of the Bible, it is said of Joseph the following: "Genesis 3939 And the LORD was with Joseph, and he was a prosperous man, and he was in the house of his master the Egyptian."
- *Supernatural performances:* You can do things that, by your power, you cannot achieve when God is upon you. He does through you breakthroughs and acceleration of victories beyond the realm of this physical world. As Judges 15:14, the Bible in the Kings version, too, says that the Spirit of the LORD came upon Samson with strength, which he needed to break the ropes and chains and kill the Philistine.
- *Safeguarding:* God keeps you safe from dangers, catastrophes, and enmity of individuals and even remakes all things to advance your benefit—in specific, hidden ways. As Psalm 91:4 (KJV) says, "I will abide in thy tabernacle for ever: I will trust in the covert of thy wings." He holds in the palm of his hand a safe and secure place.

Being God's chosen or having God's hand upon your life is an indication of divine presence, direction, blessing, deliverance, and assistance to trade as and when he wills it in blessings awaiting you. It is the revealed power of God at work for you, turning you around by the operation of the Holy Spirit within you. God's hand delivers you from constraints and assailants to show you the vast plans and programs vested in you.

The Hand Of God's Favor

The hand of God indicates His blessings, protection, and power over one's life. Every time a man tries to walk in obedience to God and attempt to do His will, there is strength in His hand to protect and bless that man and lead him.

The hand of God working at the right time in people's lives to guide, protect, or supply for them is an Old Testament theme. For instance, when the Israelites were trapped between the Red Sea and Pharaoh's advancing army, God parted the waters with His hand so they could escape (Exodus 14:21 KJV): And Moses stretched forth his hand toward the sea, and the Lord turned the sea into a strong east wind all night, and the Lord made the waters dry land and the water be divided. It saves them from being destroyed through the providence of God's hand.

Similarly, when the prophet Elijah was struggling with depression and fear, God sent an angel to feed him bread that would sustain him for his journey: And as he lay and slept in a valley to the south of Jebqu, and there was a juniper tree, behold, the angel came unto him and said to him, Arise, and eat. And he looked, and, behold, there was a cake baked on the coals and a cruse of water at his head" (1 Kings 19:5-6 KJV). Knowing very well what the man required, the hand of God supplied it to Elijah.

We also notice the favor/protection that God bestows on Esther, Daniel Joseph, and others. When Esther risked her life to save her people, the Jews, "the king held out to Esther the golden scepter that was in his hand" as a gesture of goodwill and acceptance (Esther 5:2 KJV). The king's scepter saved her from being executed, which conveyed the message God favored her. When Daniel was thrown into the lions' den for refusing to stop praying, God sent an angel to shut the lions' mouths and protect Daniel (Daniel 6:22). And when Joseph was sold into slavery by his brothers, "the Lord was with Joseph, and he was a prosperous man" even in adverse circumstances (Genesis 39:2).

These examples are that God helps and protects them and puts His blessings for His people. We know that no matter how difficult the times get, we will not be left on our own. The Bible reminds us that "the hand of our God is upon all them for good that seek him" (Ezra 8:22 KJV). His hand covers all those who seek Him in a genuine manner.

Form a habit of praying for peace or prayer for protection when we are overwhelmed by anxiety or afraid. The Psalms describe God as "my rock and my fortress" as well as "my high tower" of protection (Psalm 18:2, 144:2 KJV). There is no being on earth that can overpower God almighty.

We can also ask God to guide our ways and lead us to opportunities. Proverbs 21:1, which says, "The king's heart is in the hand of the LORD, as the rivers of water: he turneth it whithersoever he will." While people may devise their affairs, a person's life is predestined by the Lord in his calling. These two verses assure believers of the fact that no matter the circumstances in their lives, God has them in His hands firmly.

Also, we should implore for God's hand to enable us to accomplish the work he wants done on earth. In the same way that the Lord put his might in a shepherd's staff for Moses or lamps and trumpets for Gideon's army, He wishes to use his people if only they will present themselves. For example, in the old gospel song, the chorus is "Use me, Lord, use me."

Amidst the chaos that characterizes the world and exists in our fears, there is a rock that symbolizes hope with the hand of God. We are comforted by the fact that the power that created galaxies is interested in the little things that happen in our lives.

He promises to work all things together for our good because we belong to Him (Romans 8:28). It is indeed astonishing. How much authority and how much attention is in the hands of God? May we perpetually look and bow to His will and prepare to embrace His divine help, His grace always to strengthen us for each day.

Victory Over Enemies

God elevates those whom he has chosen to bless and gives them victory over their enemies, this is an act of the almighty God. This, however, carries more than just a granting of favor or protection to his own people. God desires that all people would come to repentance and salvation (2 Peter 3:9). Therefore, even when He pushes His people into an advantage over the enemies, He does it not for annihilation but for a chance to reclaim.

When the Israelites and Moses escaped Egypt and Pharaoh finally saw the pursuing armies, the people were sandwiched between the sea before them and the enemy at their heels. From this human angle, they could hardly pull through any victory. However, God acted on behalf of His people, stretching the Red Sea to provide them with a path toward freedom. Exodus 14:13-14 (KJV) When Moses said to the people, Fear not, stand still, you will see the salvation of the Lord going on today; for the Egyptians you see today, none will see again for ever. When this happens, he also reminds them, saying, *"The Lord shall fight for you, and you shall hold your peace."* By this great act of might, the LORD left no doubt in anyone's mind as to who owned the war. He reached for the win and released the enemy's control with his hand.

But even in this deliverance, God was not wholly hardhearted to those who rose against his people. While Pharaoh's armies seemed intent on killing the defenseless Israelites, nothing indicated that God wanted them totally destroyed. By this show of his might, the Lord glorified Himself; Pharaoh's heart remained obstinate, and the Israelites received their deliverance. But Scripture says some

Egyptians feared God's power and escaped the sea (Exodus 14:31). That too was evident when God delivered the Israel people victory; He even spared his mercy to those who would recompense.

We are fellow recipients of the gracious favor of God, which mandates the people of God to be compassionate, even to the enemy. Proverbs 25:21-22 KJV, "*If thine enemy is hungry, give him bread to eat; and if he is thirsty, give him water to drink: For thou shalt heap coals of fire upon his head, and the LORD shall reward thee.*" Instead, the people of God should respond with the heart of redemption to combat violence instead of violence. Showing unusual love is an example that a believer gives to the world. It creates a vacuum for Him to act in people's lives, to swap hatred for healing.

When God gives his people extraordinary power and ability over their enemies, it places his people in a category over the enemies. Enemies that a nation has brought low can be near that nation and receive from the people of the nation a revelation of the living God, just as Joseph's brethren, who sold him down into Egypt, had to bow before him later on.

Joseph's brothers had a clear and malicious plan to harm him, but God was using circumstances to provide Joseph leadership to bring forgiveness rather than vengefulness. Even though he experienced injustice of the highest degree, Joseph himself was very merciful. As he told his brothers, "*Fear not, for am I in the place of God? But as for you, ye thought evil against me; but God meant it unto good, to bring to pass, as it is this day, to save many people alive*" (Genesis 50:19-20). Joseph also prefigures Christ, who is a Savior by death. Instead of throwing the fury God so rightly deserved, his people exercised power gently with the intention to save.

This means that for the members and believers, God has the final say on victory whenever there are such forms of opposition. But this victory does not perform only this function. In this way, placing His people in the supernatural, God ensures they open blind eyes to His mercy. Religious enemies can thus be said to become friends and indeed become siblings. When granted power over enemies, God's people carry the reconciliation ministry in clay vessels (2 Corinthians 4:7-9). We are ambassadors of whom enemies may obtain knowledge and change from evil to good. There's always redemption with God. He uses all things for the good of those saved, including people overcoming their oppressors. His divine hand exalts the meek, even those who love their enemies, through blessed abundance to defeat it.

God's Hand In Your Future

God became involved in your future to guarantee that you succeed and your destiny is protected. When His hand is on you, it means that He is leading you, shielding you, and positioning events for you. The Bible verse Jeremiah 29:11 gives information about the action plan of God: the word of the Lord, 'I know the plans I have intended for you.' I want you to have peace and a promising future that will be full of hope for you, my people. With that hand, every speculation is controlled to the precise degree necessary to make the destiny He chose for you materialize.

God's hand not only opens doors to take you to much more than you ever hoped for but also protects you from worse things. Psalm 37:23-24 reads, "The LORD orders the steps of a good man: and he delighteth in his way. Though he fall, he shall not be utterly cast down: for the LORD upholdeth him with his hand." If they stumble, they won't face first into the floor because the Lord is prepared to catch them. It also holds you and assures you that no matter the obstacles that may come your way, you will overcome them and continue forward.

Besides this, the power of God's hand provides you with the necessary wisdom, strength, and resources needed to perform your task. As you believe God, He orients your life's seasons to get you closer to the divine destiny outlined for you; your destiny is guarded against the advances of the enemy, and you are directed into those divine purposes.

There are nice things in store for your future through the power that made you. He reportedly wants you to do well and to be protected. When God's hand is on you, He is leading you and teaching you about right and wrong. Yes, it works, for he is doing only good things, not for himself but for you.

Another is that God oversees the small things in your life. He creates opportunities and shields you from risks. If there are issues, God often ensures you do not stay stuck in that particular moment.

God also meets your needs—the needs to accomplish that purpose —for wisdom, strength, and resources. If you trust God, He will use all the stages in life to lead you to His intended success for your life. He protects you from enemies and ushers you right into His blessings.

Therefore, God's hand is planning and working to design an incredible future for you. He leads, guards, supplies, and arranges for you; he orchestrates events in your best interest. Whenever you fall, He picks you back up and sets you back on the path you were on before. He is leading you to His positive future for you in store. You can commit your life today and all your tomorrows into His mighty hands.

Standing Strong In God's Favor

Life has a way of offering trials, which may lead to feelings of loss and failure. That is why the Bible clearly explains that when we believe in God and try to live the life He wants us to live, we can never fail or be overcome. As Psalm 37:23-24 (KJV) says, "*The steps of a good man are ordered by the LORD: and he delighteth in his way. Though he fall, he shall not be utterly cast down: for the*

LORD upholdeth him with his hand." This verse reveals that if we are Christ, we will not fall or miss the mark, and if we do, God will hold us up with His righteous right hand if we are doing what is right.

How can followers of God have this conviction that they cannot be conquered? This is true since one of the most significant reasons for the continuing need for Christ is that God has not changed. The Bible says, *"Jesus Christ is the same yesterday and today and forever"* (Hebrews 13:8, KJV). The attributes above of God: love, mercy, justice, and faithfulness do not change. So, His promises and words over our lives have also stood forever. The miracle is that if He has promised to cause us to triumph, that promise will never fail, no matter what situations come against us.

Not only is God eternal, but His intention and His purpose also abide from one generation to the next. As Isaiah 46:10 (KJV) says, *"Declaring the end from the beginning, and from ancient times the things that are not yet done, saying, My counsel shall stand, and I will do all my pleasure."* Jesus also declares in Matthew 24:35 (KJV), *"Heaven and earth shall pass away, but my words shall not pass away."* From the above verses, it is evident that God was already predestined before the advancement of time. We can do nothing that will hinder what God has planned for our future. If He says we will succeed at some endeavor or triumph over adversity, nothing from the realm of evil or even the natural can hinder it.

In other words, we should learn to hear God's voice to apply this assurance of victory in our everyday lives. The better acquainted we become with His nature through reading the scripture, the better we can understand what He says when He speaks over our situations. As Jesus said in John 10:27 (KJV), "My sheep hear my voice, and I know them, and they follow me." When we have taken the time to learn about Jesus as our shepherd, it becomes easier to tell whether a given thought in the mind is from Him. So, listening to His voice repeatedly builds our spirit to counter any words of negative power, such as defeat or failure.

We also receive these favorable promises by bringing our minds and tongues into agreement with what God is saying about us rather than being led by what our emotions are saying to us. If God says, we are victorious, but we say, "*I just feel like a failure; the devil has lied to us.*" Suppose we follow that thinking and allow our minds to ponder on it. In that case, we are accepting the lie of the enemy when we say, 'I must have missed God.' 2 Corinthians 10:5 (KJV) directs us to "*Casting down imaginations, and every high thing that exalteth itself against the knowledge of God, and bringing into captivity every thought to the obedience of Christ.*" That means we must intentionally decide to focus on what the Word of God has to say as far as being vital in His might and overcoming power when thoughts of defeat come.

We must remember that walking in a manner deserving of victory does not guarantee that one will not stumble or go through trials in a campaign. In those situations, with God's help, we can deal with and move on to making the Kingdom of God a reality. As much as you suffered affliction just like Job did, the Lord can restore it to you mightily, bring forth the same character in you, and make us fruitful for the Lord's glory.

Thus, the people who follow Jesus can be confident that just as God has been faithful in their executing righteous purposes since the days of old, He also desires to prove Himself faithful to present His righteous purposes to us. As we decide daily to worship Him, accept His point of view concerning our lives, and obey His instructions, He will exalt us with His righteousness right hand to enable us to fulfill his plans for our lives. Though trials will come, we must remember that with Christ, we are ultimately more than conquerors if God be for us (Romans 8:37, KJV). Built on that firm foundation, we can remain in favor today and forever.

CHAPTER SEVEN

WALKING IN DIVINE POWER

"**W**alk in divine power" means living a life of power and dominion daily. It means that you are of advantage of the Spirit. Only the power of God allows one to live such a life. Christ promised his disciples that they were going to receive this power. He said, "But ye shall receive power, after that the Holy Ghost is come upon you." (Acts 1:8 KJV). Through this power, believers can enjoy a victorious life, come to victory over the testing, and have victorious Christian service in the Lord's Kingdom.

What is this divine power? First, it is the power to deal with sin. All believers in Jesus were sinful in the past, but not anymore. Alone, we lose time and again. But God sanctifies us from the heart, which is inside a person, through the Spirit. The Spirit empowers us to avoid sin and wrong decisions and actions. Therefore, our sinful nature is subdued as we submit to the Spirit. We are empowered to live a holy life.

Divine power deals with fear. We are all afraid of something, failure, rejection, the future, and even people. But "*For God hath not given us the spirit of fear; but of power, and love, and a sound mind.*" (2 Timothy 1:7 NKJV). The kind of love that he has revealed is perfect, and this kind of love is casting out fear. When we spend time with Jesus, walking with him as he teaches us, hearing the words he has to say, and most of all, being aware that he accepts us as we are, our fears go away. His loud mouth brings us assurance and courage.

This power reigns over all the forces that might be opposed to it overtly but also those that might covertly resist change. Christians have an adversary who seeks to sabotage our faith, trust, and confidence in God as our Lord and Savior. However, the power of the Holy Spirit is a factor for us and even wages war on our behalf. He protects our hearts and our minds. He tells lies and exaggerates the details. He unmasks the conspiracies against them. God's power is available to the believer by faith and prayer, and no weapon formed against the believer will stand.

To walk in divine power is to say that we are living instruments in the hand of the Divine, through which God demonstrates his power and glory. We are like Jesus Christ here on earth, with God's power empowering us to do compassionate works, healing, justice, and deliverance. Christians meet the living God through us. Thus, when we surrender to the Spirit's control of our words and actions, God turns them into miracles. People get saved, and their lives are changed by the power of the apostle working through them.

How, then, are we to live perpetually in divine power? Two essential practices keep us connected to the source: Engaging ourselves daily with the Word of God by reading, hearing, and praying to God throughout the day. Jesus explained: "If ye abide in me, and my words abide in you, ye shall ask what ye will, and it shall be done unto you." (John 15:7 KJV). While we walk closely with Jesus, marinate our minds in God's Word, and practice communicating all things to Him in prayer, we never disconnect ourselves from the power of the Spirit. The fruit that remains in our lives is not because of our work but through the grace and help of God. As the prophet Zechariah declared about serving God: *"Then he answered and spake unto me, saying, This is the word of the LORD unto Zerubbabel, saying, Not by might, nor by power, but by my spirit, saith the LORD of hosts."* (Zachariah 4:6 KJV)

Consequently, walking in divine power brings deep permanency through our lifestyle, spoken words, and actions. We take the authority of the Kingdom of God into every realm of life—family, workplace, ministry, and civil. As we submit ourselves completely to and yield to his leadership, he changes, heals, redeems, and liberates people and geographical locations bound by sin and evil. We carry out the will of God regarding his miracles and wonders on the face of the earth.

Living In The Fullness Of God's Power

The power and blessing of God simply depict the authority, controlling authority, and favor that belong to born-again identities through the shed blood of Jesus. Salvation from sin, forgiveness of sins, deliverance from the devil, access to God— but our strength as Christians lies in the blood that Jesus spilled on the cross. By the blood of Jesus Christ, we are redeemed, and sin, along with death, has been conquered. Revelation 12:11 says, *"And they overcame him by the blood of the Lamb, and by the word of their testimony, and they loved not their lives unto the death."* This demonstrates an ability to live in victory despite the devil through shedding Christ's blood.

So, walking in authority simply means identifying yourself in Christ. You were born not of your own decision but by the purpose of God. You are a child of God because the blood of Jesus has washed you and given you the right to unleash Jesus' authority over sin, hatred, or anything anti-life. In Luke 19:10, KJV, we are made to understand that power was given unto us to tread on serpents and scorpions, meaning we are in charge of the devil.

The blood of Jesus also opens us to divine approval, favor, or access to God's blessings and grace; we can do so fearlessly. Ephesians 1:7 in the KJV says, *"In whom we have redemption through his blood, the forgiveness of sins, according to the riches of his grace."* Thus, living fully in this power from God, we are walking in favor, authority, and control to accomplish God's purpose for our lives.

Therefore, We must stay reminded that the power in us is not ours, but it is from God. So victory and blessing are possible only because of what Jesus did on the cross. This means that as we maintain fellowship with Him through prayers, fellowshipping, and studying the word, the power of Jesus will expand through us. This will look different for each person; however, two primary strategies are worth following: For some, it means fearlessly casting down their pearls before the swine; that's evangelism. For some, it may imply happily helping the less fortunate in our society. There are so many ways we can allow the power of God to be manifested through us.

Therefore, the most crucial thing in this case is that we should walk in love. The scripture is unequivocal in reminding us that that which we do should be done out of love. As 1 Corinthians 13:2 KJV states, "*And though I have the gift of prophecy, and understand all mysteries, and all knowledge; and though I have all faith, so that I could remove mountains, and have not charity, I am nothing.*" This power that comes from God should not puff us up but draw people towards Christ.

Regarding morality, living in the fullness of God's power means living an upright life. Praise and favor of the Lord are not to be earned by mending one's ways to be perfect. But as believers, we want to do it in a manner that glorifies Him to the best of our abilities. Romans 12:1 states in the KJV that having been bought with a price, we are to present our bodies as a "*living sacrifice, holy, acceptable unto God.*" Of course, we make mistakes and do not give up; the Lord helps us rise and continue our journey to be holy.

Miracles, Signs, And Wonders

Wonders, signs, and miracles are divine acts that reveal God's presence and his might. Therefore, Christians can tap into this power through faith in the crucifixion and the received Holy Spirit. When Jesus died, His blood was shed to forgive our sins, giving us direct access to God the Father (Hebrews 10:19-22, KJV). The holy Scripture affirms, *But if the spirit of Him that raised Jesus from the dead dwells in you, he that raised Christ from the dead shall also quicken your mortal bodies by his spirit that dwelleth in you.* (Romans 8:11, KJV). Therefore, as children of God, we bear His authority and power to perform signs to His glory.

There are specific examples of miracles, signs, and wonders that believers can do through the power of the Spirit. Among all the healings, physical healings are the most frequent. Jesus healed all kinds of sickness and disease (Matthew 4:23–24). He then commissioned His followers to do the same works He did (John 14:12). This was when Peter and John met a lame beggar, and using the name Jesus, they said to him, Rise and walk. Immediately, his feet and ankles were strengthened, and he began to leap and praise God (Acts 3:1-8). The people receiving this miracle reacted the same way and glorified God. Whenever we pray for the afflicted and are answered by the healing power of God, God is glorified, and men witness miracles.

One other significant way believers exhibit God's miracle-working power is through deliverance from the effect of the devil. Many accounts of people being delivered from mental anguish, drug and alcohol dependence, sickness, etc., are challenging an unbeliever with authority in the name of Jesus to leave. The 72 disciples went through this when Jesus began to send them to preach the gospel, and he said to them, "And the seventy returned with joy, saying, Lord, even the devils are subject unto us through thy name." Luke 10:17, KJV). Authority over the workings of evil demonstrates that Jesus is more excellent than Satan and fails, bringing joy and freedom.

Another significant category of miracles is the category of

supernatural supply. God promises to supply all our needs according to His riches in glory (Philippians 4:19), and everyone has countless stories of unmerited divine provision or miraculous financial windfalls. Some common examples that anybody would have come across may be getting money from an unexpected source just in time to pay a bill or not running out of food stock while food stamps arrive late. Blessing prayers for provision break the ground for the resourcefulness of God as a Provider to His beloved.

The only way for believers to assert this power is by drawing nearer to Him. This begins by believing in salvation through Christ, which leads to our being reclaimed by the Father. We, therefore, need to get acquainted with Him through prayer, worship, reading His word, and following His instruction and guidance through the Holy Spirit. This is because as we surrender ourselves fully to the Spirit, more of heaven is set free on the earth.

Signs, wonders, and miracles: The operational mandate is very demanding because the emphasis is on God and not on merely amazing the people. He [Jesus] would frequently warn the beneficiaries of the miracles not to spread the good news. Instead of offering examples of people who brag about the supernatural, we need to lead everyone to find Jesus Christ and his saving grace. Serving as pipelines of power, we don't exchange a single step lightly and wholly depend on the Spirit for direction.

Therefore, the Christ believers have an opportunity and a right to hunt the miracle power in the redemptive blood of Jesus and the Person of the Holy Spirit. In other words, the more intimate and obedient we become to God, the more Himself will perform marvelous miracles through us. This is expressed in occasions such as healing, deliverance, miraculous supply, and other manifestations of an unseen kingdom creeping into this world. May the eyes of each reader of this article be opened to see it.

The Practical Glory Of God

The 'glory' of God is simply the fact that His nature and presence are made known, and we are practically living witness to this power. This glorifies God and witnesses His ability and action in us to those near us.

You can show the Lord's glory through good work done to the best of the person's abilities. This is because when we work, we do so with dedication, integrity, and skill, presenting the creator's character. Colossians 3:23 KJV states, "*And whatsoever ye do, do it heartily, as to the Lord, and not unto men.*" The scripture plainly instructs Christians to do their work for the Lord and not hide that he will reward everyone for what they do. As we put our effort in this manner, it is pleasurable to God and glorifying. Everyone may pay attention to how we do our work—the integrity, completeness, and enthusiasm we imprint—and wonder where such spirit comes from. That creates a chance to clarify that it is God's power within.

As we all go about our ordinary jobs, we can serve God in and through our daily work; second, He may show His glory through signs and wonders, which He can perform through us beyond our standard capabilities. Philippians 4:13 For all things are possible to the one who strengthens me, as it is written: "*I can do all things through Christ which strengtheneth me.*" (KJV). If we surrender ourselves to Him and trust not in our strength, He may enable us to deal with what seems impossible alone. This is how His power might be made clear through the tenderness of praise to Him. For instance, a person with undesirable habits may look and find God endowing them with strange abilities to combat something that, in their human strength, they could not fight. If God intercedes to alter and transform the impossible by our efforts, then God shall be glorified.

The Lord can also reveal His glory in meeting our mundane

necessities of life. When we look to God as our provider and trust Him to meet our needs according to His riches in glory (Philippians 4:19), He may choose to answer in ways that are entirely unexpected and demonstrate His loving care and might within the situation. He can fix it so you're inundated with blessings—he gives you this and meets your financial needs in a way you did not anticipate! As these provision miracles accumulate, the following that results from our positive assertion that God is providing for us causes those who witness those consistent daily provisions to ask where they could be coming from. Finally, and in conclusion, the glory goes to God, 'the great giver.'

Besides His blessings, we also glorify God with a loud shout of praise in suffering. When we are in trials but turn around and rejoice and give thanks in the midst, God has made our sufficiency. His presence and promises hold on to us even at that time when things are tough. This is why people might find it incredibly astonishing to see someone with real problems act excitedly and offer compliments instead of complaining. It can only be suggestive of the working of God in our midst. When others notice our supernatural peace, hope, and faith, even in the painful state, God is at work. This brings Him honor.

Of course, while God can do it through us, He always gets the glory for such an act of power. Therefore, we should be extremely wary of ever attempting to claim credit for ourselves for what He has done for us or use His power the way one would use a hammer. We are just called to go through the process of living as He directs so that He may be glorified in us. We walk gently in yielded, humble, and willing spirits so that His daily strength and character can be manifested in *daily* tasks. As that happens, our lives testify about the great God we worship and serve. He has been using us to showcase His existence through our everyday operations from Mondays to Fridays, and all this glorifies His name.

Carrying God's Favor Daily

Every day, when one wakes up, it becomes really overwhelming to get up and do the tasks or face the challenges that come with the day. Money issues, disease, family drama—the world is oppressive, with anxiety and fear everywhere. Yet, as children of God, we have a powerful weapon against all darkness: the acknowledgment that we live by faith in the favor which God has bestowed upon us.

Now, I want to learn what it means to have the favor of God. This is the understanding that the Lord of the entire creation is for you, interceding for you, and has a beautiful future. As Psalm 5:12 (KJV) says, *"For thou, LORD, wilt bless the righteous; with favor wilt thou compass him as with a shield."* God wraps Himself around us, so no matter what our struggles or wars might appear, He lavishes us with grace, mercy, and blessings.

Being in this kind of confidence gives life a new day and hope instead of asking, 'What next?' When challenges arise, we remember that God's strength will see us through, just as David wrote in Psalm 28:7 (KJV): *"The LORD is my strength, and my shield; my heart trusted in him, and I am helped: therefore my heart greatly rejoiceth; and with my song will I praise him."* This knowledge is evidence of grace from the Almighty God, creating room for peace and courage to take root in the heart.

How can we practically demonstrate that we are carrying God's favor in our daily lives? Praying before starting the day and reading a verse of good Scripture sets a better spiritual foundation in the morning. Dedicating precious moments in a day to say thank you to Him for having His hand in your life is fulfilling and helps you remain spiritually sensitive. Speaking words of hope and encouragement to others is a way of shining the light of His grace around all of you.

The more we realize how often God loves us, the deeper it embeds and reorients itself within and through us. In wrapping up the argument, God's favor transforms into an indispensable robe of assurance we can take off at leisure. It opposes anxiety and despair before they set their roots. It cannot but glow before men and women living in the darkness who require the light of his grace.

We all fall and err—this cannot be refuted as it goes against the grain of our real life. However, sins, mistakes, or lack of self-worth must not hide that God loves his people. *"For I am persuaded that neither death nor life...nor any other creature shall be able to separate us from the love of God"* (Romans 8:38-39, KJV). Stay true to this favor, dear. The dead are hoping for the gift Jesus came to bring.

If you wake up each day feeling so thankful and happy, then you know that heaven has fully blessed you. When action takes place due to a feeling of ultimate ease, knowing that all things will be okay despite the current circumstances, that is grace. God's grace illuminates your life so that you meet the day's events with hope and a sense of purpose.

If there is a divine favor, then all the problems are solved. As you need, solutions come through when we least expect them; they just come through right on time. You end up with the right messages to the right audience for the help you need or the service being sought. Real-life feelings steer you prudently through choices, big and small. Openings occur, opportunities come your way, and you glide effortlessly through hurdles that hitherto posed as barriers or challenges.

The essence of living under heaven's blessings involves maintaining an openness, willingness, or trust as to heaven's dispensations. When one builds his paradigm from God's provisions of certainty instead of lack, they set up the internal conditions for manifestations of favor. Your role is passive; you are to accept what you are given today with an open heart.

The blessings of God are as sure as the rain and the sunshine and are received by all alike. However, for those who consciously bring awareness of divine favor, it becomes easier for them to notice the gifts within their midst at every moment. Program yourself to look for and anticipate little miracles, and there will be more of such miracles.

With the help of grace, the products of leisure and prosperity can enrich all of your programs. Go through each obligation with a dance instead of dragging your feet. Perform ordinary tasks with grace and productivity to ensure that time and energy spill over for the 'good things.' May 'favor' realign you from the glow of scarcity to the abundance of plenitude so you may glory in the opportunity to bless others by enriching your own 'fulfilled' sources.

It also signifies receiving a blessing from God, which makes one view life as full of opportunities and, hence, a worthy life. It's a dance with Providence where one responds to the divine call and plays an influential role in conjunction with the spiritual power to serve one's highest interest. Casting our worries unto the Lord, there is beauty in every hour, every minute, and every second. Always stand with your heart wide open and your feet on the ground to live that grace into the new day, affirming the favor of God inside and out.

CONCLUSION

The Blood's Eternal Echo

T he powerful resonance of Jesus Christ's blood releases a profound echo that transcends time and situation. This timeless echo offers consolation, hope, and serenity for the anxious, afraid, and worried. God's gift of true peace comes from the blood spilled on Calvary's cross.

In a world of turmoil, inner and outer peace is precious. The blood of Jesus provides this peace, liberating us from fear, worry, and doubt. *"And, having made peace through the blood of his cross, by him to reconcile all things unto himself"* (Colossians 1:20, KJV). Through faith in Jesus, we experience a clean slate, and peace with God becomes our reality.

The blood of Jesus not only reconciles us to God but also speaks peace into every aspect of our lives. As our spirits unite with God, His peace permeates our hearts, minds, and circumstances. The blood's voice reassures us, speaking words of comfort, hope, and peace.

In moments of stress or overwhelm, invoking the power of Jesus's blood brings the cross's transformative power to mind. *"Peace I leave with you, my peace I give unto you: not as the world giveth, give I unto you. Let not your heart be troubled, neither let it be afraid"* (John

14:27, KJV). This peace guards our hearts and minds, granting liberty from doubt and assurance to follow God's will.

The blood's eternal echo cancels restrictions, hindrances, and fears, empowering believers to advance in God's purpose. Claiming the blood's power addresses struggles directly, encouraging the voice of Scripture. The blood promises strength, favor, and blessing.

As born-again Christians, understanding the authority of Jesus's blood is crucial for a life without restrictions. Invoking the blood's wonder-working power opens possibilities of peace, purpose, and spiritual breakthroughs.

The blood of Jesus liberates us from confinement and speaks of God's love and presence. It declares, "Let there be light, order, and triumph." Amidst life's challenges, listen to the blood's eternal echo, speaking words of hope, life, and peace.

www.ingramcontent.com/pod-product-compliance
Lightning Source LLC
Chambersburg PA
CBHW071905020426
42331CB00010B/2675